■SCHOLASTIC

Fluency-Building Around the Year

15 Reproducible Read-Aloud Plays That Help Students Build Fluency and Deepen Comprehension–All Year Long!

D0887195

New York • Toronto • London • Auckland • Sydney
Mexico City • New Delhi • Hong Kong • Buenos Aires

Teaching *Resources*

Scholastic Inc. grants teachers permission to photocopy the plays from this book for classroom use. No other part of this publication may be reproduced in whole or in part, or stored in a retrieval system, or transmitted in any form or by any means, electronic, mechanical, photocopying, recording, or otherwise, without written permission of the publisher. For information regarding permission, write to Scholastic Inc., 557 Broadway, New York, NY 10012-3999.

This adaptation of *Plays Around the Year* © Scholastic, 1994, features plays by:
Robin Bernard, Jim Halverson, Cass Hollander, Bobbi Katz, Deborah Kovacs, Tara McCarthy,
Carol Pugliano-Martin, Liza Charlesworth, Eve Spencer, Paula Thomas, and Sandra Widener.

Cover design by Brian LaRossa
Cover and interior illustration by Jane Conteh-Morgan

ISBN-13 978-0-545-12474-4
ISBN-10 0-545-12474-3

Introduction 5

    What Is Fluency? 5

    Using the Plays to Build Fluency 6

    Assessing Fluency 8

    Meeting the Language Arts Standards 9

    Teacher Rubric for Assessing Oral Fluency. 10

    Student Checklist for Oral Reading 11

Fall

Rhymes to the Rescue
(Back to School) 12

Planting Seeds, Spreading Sunshine
(Johnny Appleseed's Birthday) 21

The Hidden Corn
(Hispanic Heritage Month). 29

The Ugly Pumpkin
(Halloween). 36

A Native American Welcome
(Thanksgiving) 43

Winter

The Hesitant Hibernator
(Animals in Winter) 50

The Mystery of the Missing Munchies
(Winter Holidays) 58

Kindness, the Magic Peacekeeper
(Chinese New Year) 65

Big Words, Strong Words
(Martin Luther King, Jr. Day) 73

Dreaming of George and Abe
(Presidents' Day) 80

Spring

An Earth Day Carol
(Earth Day) 89

Becoming a Butterfly
(Life Cycles) 97

A Kindness Returned
(Be Kind to Animals Week) 104

Betsy Ross, Seamstress With a Mission
(Flag Day) 110

Summer Dreams
(End of School) 119

Introduction

Welcome to *Fluency-Building Plays Around the Year*. Plays are a wonderful vehicle for learning and building reading skills, and this book offers you a year's worth of read-aloud plays to use with your class. The 15 plays are designed to complement themes and celebrations throughout the year, and help students build key fluency skills and deepen comprehension. (To see how the plays connect to key language arts standards, see page 9.)

At the start of each play are helpful Teaching Notes designed both to simplify and enhance sharing the plays with your students. The Teaching Notes provide essential background information in a quick collection of facts that introduce the play and its content. You'll also find Extension Activities that offer suggestions for activities to help you link the plays to your curriculum year-round and to broaden the play experience for your students.

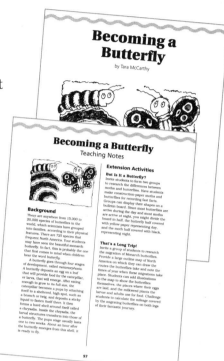

What Is Fluency?

In his book *The Fluent Reader* (Scholastic, 2003), Timothy Rasinski writes: "Reading fluency refers to the ability of readers to read quickly, effortlessly, and efficiently with good, meaningful expression." As Rasinski and other researchers note, fluency is about much more than merely reading accurately. A fluent reader can recognize words automatically and read them smoothly and rapidly. This ability, known as "automaticity," plays an important role in comprehension (LaBerge and Samuels, 1974 as cited in Blevins, 2001). A certain amount of cognitive energy is involved in reading, whether aloud or to oneself. It makes sense that if students spend less energy on decoding, they have more to spend on comprehension and meaning. And when students are able to focus on comprehension and meaning, they can infuse words and phrases with expression, making sense of the text. Nonfluent reading is often marked by choppiness, as students concentrate on each word rather than the meaning of an entire phrase (Samuels, 1979 as cited in Blevins, 2001). Thus, a student may be able to decode words with accuracy but still not be a fluent reader. In addition to automaticity, reading with fluency involves these essential skills:

Prosody: the ability to read a text orally using appropriate pitch, tone, and rhythm

Phrasing: linking words together into phrases marked by appropriate pauses

Rate: the pace at which one reads

Intonation: the expressive emphasis given to particular words or phrases

Fluent reading does not necessarily come "naturally" along with students' growing ability to accurately decode text. In fact, scientifically based research studies (Chard, Vaughn & Tyler, 2002; Kuhn & Stahl, 2000; National Institute of Child Health and Development, 2000, as cited in Rasinski, 2004) have shown that direct and explicit fluency lessons are an essential part of any literacy program. In its 2000 report, the National Reading Panel indicated that fluency should be a key component of effective instruction.

So how, then, do we teach fluent reading effectively? A number of factors come into play. Of course, it is important to practice repeated readings of texts: The more times students see and hear the text, the more "automatic" it becomes (Samuels, 1979 as cited in Blevins, 2001). Plays easily lend themselves to repeated reading since they are meant to be rehearsed and to be read aloud.

Using the Plays to Build Fluency

The length and reading level of the plays make them well suited for fluency practice—so important for building reading comprehension. The plays contain a range of punctuation and phrasing, two key elements of fluency. For example, in Rhymes to the Rescue (page 13), An Earth Day Carol (page 90), and Summer Dreams (page 120), some of the speaking parts include a line-by-line arrangement of rhyming verses that helps children identify phrase boundaries.

Introducing the Plays

Review words that may be unfamiliar or difficult for students to read. Discuss strategies students can use to decode words they do not know, such as finding beginning or ending sounds, and breaking the word into parts. Provide background for any concepts in the plays that might be unfamiliar to students.

Read a play aloud several times while students follow along. Model how pacing, expression, punctuation and inflection help communicate meaning. For example, to demonstrate how punctuation affects expression and meaning, write the same sentence from a play three times on chart paper, first using a period, then an exclamation point, and finally, a question mark.

> A whole pile of corn. Yippee.
>
> A whole pile of corn! Yippee!
>
> A whole pile of corn? Yippee?
>
> (From The Hidden Corn, page 30)

Read each sentence aloud and ask students to describe how your voice changed with each reading. How does this change the meaning? Repeat the demonstration and then invite students to read aloud with you.

Choral and Echo Reading

Choral and echo reading are effective techniques for giving students the repeated practice they need to build fluency. To do choral reading, you and your students read together as a group. This encourages students to read at the same pace and with the same phrasing and intonation as the rest of the group. In echo reading, you read a line and students then repeat it, echoing your expression, tone, and pacing.

Readers Theater

Readers Theater is an excellent way to build fluency. This technique also allows all students to participate and succeed. English Language Learners, in particular, benefit from listening to the repeated readings of the text by other students. And as group members work together on fluency skills such as expression, intonation, and phrasing, they can offer each other feedback and encouragement. Students often feel more comfortable exploring new characters and experimenting

Teaching Tips

❖ Have students use a highlighter to distinguish their speaking parts and lines.

❖ After each group has performed a play, have students switch parts. This will provide expanded fluency practice by allowing students to experience different characters and varied punctuation, phrasing, and intonation. It will also give students a chance to enjoy reading large roles as well as small ones and, at the same time, ensure that each student gets adequate reading time for fluency practice.

with different voices without the burden of memorizing lines or movements.

To prepare for Readers Theater, divide the class into groups. Give a copy of the play to each student. Assign the different speaking parts or have group members choose them together. Tell each group to read and rehearse their play many times. Give students plenty of practice time, reminding them to pay attention to the reading behaviors they learned. Once the members of a group feel confident with their reading, invite them to perform the play for the rest of the class.

Resources

For more on assessing fluency, consult these sources:

❧ *Assessing Reading Fluency* by Timothy V. Rasinski (Pacific Resources for Education and Learning, May 2004)

❧ *Building Fluency: Lessons and Strategies for Reading Success* by Wiley Blevins (Scholastic, 2001)

❧ *Fluency Strategies for Struggling Readers* by Marcia Delany (Scholastic, 2006)

❧ *The Fluent Reader* by Timothy V. Rasinski (Scholastic, 2003)

❧ *3-Minute Reading Assessments: Word Recognition, Fluency, and Comprehension, Grades 1–4* by Timothy V. Rasinski (Scholastic, 2005)

Assessing Fluency

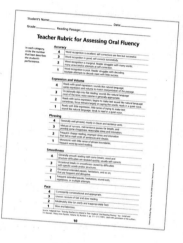

To monitor students' reading informally, ask them to read aloud and listen to how well they attend to key elements of fluency: phrasing (including intonation, stress, and pauses), volume, expression, smoothness, attention to syntax, accuracy, and pace. Use the Teacher Rubric for Assessing Oral Fluency (adapted from Zutell and Rasinski, 1991) on page 10 to track their progress. This assessment allows you to focus on specific aspects of fluency and to note areas in which students have strengths or are in need of further instruction and practice. (When using this rubric, it is helpful to listen to students do a reading several times and evaluate each element separately.) On the scale, scores range between 5 and 20. A student who scores 10 or above is progressing well; scores below 10 signal that a student's reading fluency needs to improve.

Reading specialist Marcia Delany recommends involving students in this process as well. In her book, *Fluency Strategies for Struggling Readers*, she writes, "The more you use the language of fluency, the more focus and attention you draw to the specific expectations you have of your readers and the more consciously and effectively they can work on skills in those areas." Provide students with copies of the Student Checklist for Oral Reading on page 11, model how to use it, and then encourage students to monitor their own reading patterns and progress. At the bottom of the checklist, have students record by number the areas in which they need to improve. (Students might also team up with partners and use the checklist to assess each other's reading.)

Meeting the Language Arts Standards

Mid-continent Research for Education and Learning (McRel), a nationally recognized, nonprofit organization has compiled and evaluated national and state PreK–12 curriculum standards—and proposed what teachers should provide for their students to grow proficient in language arts, among other curriculum areas. The plays and activities in this book support the following standards for students in grades 2–3.

Reading

❖ Uses self-correction strategies (for example, searches for cues, identifies miscues, rereads, asks for help)

❖ Reads aloud familiar texts with fluency and expression (for example, rhythm, flow, meter, tempo, pitch, tone, intonation)

❖ Understands the author's purpose or point of view

❖ Uses meaning clues to aid in comprehension and make predictions about content

❖ Adjusts speed of reading to suit purpose and difficulty of the material

❖ Understands level-appropriate reading vocabulary (for example, synonyms, antonyms, multiple-meaning words)

❖ Uses reading skills and strategies to understand and interpret a variety of literary texts, including plays

❖ Makes connections between characters or simple events in a literary work and people or events in his or her own life

Listening and Speaking

❖ Recites and responds to familiar texts with patterns (for example, relates information to own life, describes character, setting, plot)

❖ Uses different voice level, phrasing, and intonation for different situations

❖ Uses a variety of verbal communication skills (for example, projection, tone, volume, rate, articulations, pace, phrasing)

Source: Kendall, J. S., & Marzano, R. J. (2004). *Content knowledge: A compendium of standards and benchmarks for K–12 education* (4th ed.). Aurora, CO: Mid-continent Research for Education and Learning. Online database: http://www.mcrel.org/standards-benchmarks/

Student's Name:_____ Date:_____

Grade:_____ Reading Passage:_____

Teacher Rubric for Assessing Oral Fluency

In each category, circle the number that best describes the student's performance.

Accuracy

4	Word recognition is excellent; self-corrections are few but successful.
3	Word recognition is good; self-corrects successfully.
2	Word recognition is marginal. Reader struggles with many words; many unsuccessful attempts at self-correction.
1	Word recognition is poor. Reader struggles with decoding. Multiple attempts to decode meet with little success.

Expression and Volume

4	Reads with good expression; sounds like natural language; varies expression and volume to match interpretation of the passage.
3	Occasionally slips into flat reading; sounds like natural language most of the time; voice volume is generally appropriate.
2	Reads with some expression; begins to make text sound like natural language sometimes; focus remains largely on saying the words; reads in a quiet voice.
1	Reads with little expression; little sense of trying to make text sound like natural language; tends to read in a quiet voice.

Phrasing

4	Generally well phrased, mostly in clause and sentence units.
3	Mixture of run-ons, mid-sentence pauses for breath, and possibly some choppiness; reasonable stress and intonation.
2	Frequent choppy reading; improper stress and intonation that fail to mark ends of sentences and clauses.
1	Monotonic with little sense of phrase boundaries; frequent word-by-word reading.

Smoothness

4	Generally smooth reading with some breaks; word and structure difficulties are resolved quickly; usually self-corrects.
3	Occasional breaks in smoothness caused by difficulties with specific words and/or structures.
2	Occasional extended pauses, hesitations, and so on, that are frequent and disruptive.
1	Frequent extended pauses, hesitations, sound-outs, repetitions, or multiple attempts.

Pace

4	Consistently conversational and appropriate.
3	Uneven mixture of fast and slow reading.
2	Moderately slow (or overly and inappropriately fast).
1	Slow and laborious.

Source: Adapted from "Training Teachers to Attend to Their Students' Oral Reading Fluency," by J. Zutell and T.V. Rasinski, *Theory Into Practice*, Volume 30, Number 3, pp. 211–217 (1991). Used with permission of the authors.

Student's Name:_____ Date:_____

Student Checklist for Oral Reading

		Most of the Time	Sometimes	Not Often	Hardly Ever
1	**If I get stuck on a word or it doesn't sound right, I read it again.**	☐	☐	☐	☐
2	**I try to read words I don't know.**	☐	☐	☐	☐
3	**I read smoothly without stopping after every word.**	☐	☐	☐	☐
4	**When I read, I pay attention to punctuation at the end of a sentence.**	☐	☐	☐	☐
5	**I read with expression.**	☐	☐	☐	☐

What I Need to Work on:

_____

_____

_____

_____

_____

_____

_____

Source: Adapted from *35 Rubrics & Checklists to Assess Reading and Writing* by Adele Fiderer. Scholastic, 1998. Used with permission of the author.

Rhymes to the Rescue
Teaching Notes

My name is Liz. Rhymin' is my biz!

Background

This play can serve both as an icebreaker to bring a new class together and to introduce the idea of students feeling good about themselves. This play and the following activities reinforce the idea that everyone has something valuable to contribute—and that being different can be wonderful!

Extension Activities

Who Are You?

This activity is a good way for students to find out more about their classmates. Divide the class into pairs. On the board or chart paper, create a list of information that would be fun to discover about each other such as: most and least favorite foods; hobbies; talents; favorite books; most and least favorite school activity; proudest moments; etc. Have pairs interview each other and record responses to the items on the list. Then have students use the information to write brief, descriptive paragraphs about their partners. Read the descriptions to the class and have students guess the person's name from listening to the profile.

A Class Act

Invite students to share personal skills and knowledge with the rest of the class by being the teacher for a little while! Begin by generating a list of possible lesson topics such as how to care for pets or plants, how to do arts and crafts projects, or how to speak another language, etc. After helping each interested student decide on a viable presentation, have each one develop a simple lesson plan including a list of materials and goals for the lesson, as well as a series of steps for the presentation. Suggest that students practice their lessons on family members at home. Then set aside a regular time for students to shine in class. (After preparing and presenting their lessons, students will undoubtedly appreciate all the preparation you put into yours!)

Rhyme Time

Rhyming is a favorite activity for many students; this game lets them play with rhymes. Create a list of easy-to-rhyme words, write each on a slip of paper, and place the papers in a box or bag. Divide the class into small groups. Have one student from each group select a word from the container. Set a timer for one minute, during which time each group records all the words they can think of that rhyme with their word. At the end of the minute, each group shares their results. Then, have each group recite their rhymes for the rest of the class to repeat.

Rhymes to the Rescue

by Sandra Widener

My name is Liz:
Rhymin' is my biz!

Characters

- Ms. Jordan
- Amanda
- George
- Nancy
- Luis
- Liz
- Boy 1
- Boy 2
- Rhyme-Time Kids (rest of the class)
- Girl 1
- Girl 2

Act 1

Ms. Jordan's classroom, the first day of school. Everyone is standing at the front of the room, talking.

Ms. Jordan: I see some old friends and some new faces. Let's all say hello to each other. Let's all sit in a circle on the floor.

[Everyone sits in a circle.]

Ms. Jordan: Now I want you to go around and take turns saying your name and one favorite thing you like to do.

Amanda: I'm Amanda, and I like riding my bike.

George: My name is George. I like to play baseball.

Nancy: *[shyly]* I'm Nancy, and I like to do gymnastics.

Luis: My name is Luis, and my favorite thing is to play baseball with George.

Ms. Jordan: And next to you, Luis, I see a new student. Tell us your name, please.

Liz: My name is Liz:
Rhymin' is my biz!

Ms. Jordan: *[a bit startled]* Rhyming is your 'biz?' What do you mean?

Liz: *[shrugging]* I do it all day.
When do we play?

Ms. Jordan: We'll play later today . . . er . . . I mean there's no doubt we'll be going out. *[shakes head from side to side while smiling]* Whew! This rhyming stuff catches on fast, Liz! Now let's continue our hellos.

[As the rest of the class says their introductions, Amanda and George "whisper" together while looking at Liz.]

Amanda: Rhyming's not going to catch on to me. I think Liz is weird.

George: Do you think she's really going to rhyme all day?

Amanda: If she does, I won't sit next to her. I'm not being friends with a weirdo!

Act 2

Ms. Jordan's classroom, lunchtime of the same day.

Ms. Jordan: *[doling out lunch orders]* Liz, did you order pizza for lunch?

Liz: Yes, please!
With lots of cheese!

Amanda: *[groaning]* There she goes again! Liz, can't you stop that?

Liz: But, I like to rhyme
all of the time.

Luis: Can't you just speak like a normal kid?

Liz: *[shrugging]* It's no crime
to speak in rhyme.

Amanda: Come sit with us, Nancy. We'll leave the rhyming girl to herself.

Nancy: *[whispering softly to Amanda while looking over at Liz]* Aren't we being mean?

Amanda: *[in a loud voice]* When Liz wants to be normal like us, she can sit with us.

Liz: *[muttering sadly to herself]*
Maybe I don't belong at this school.
If being me is just not cool!

Act 3

The classroom, a few days later.

Ms. Jordan: Class, I have an announcement. There's going to be a school talent show. Any class that wants to can put on an act for the whole school. A prize will be awarded to the class with the most creative presentation!

Luis: That's great! Let's go for the prize! Now, what can we do to win?

[a few moments of silence]

Amanda: I can ride my bike, and Nancy can do gymnastic tricks!

George: No, it has to be something really different. Besides, we all want a part in the show.

[The kids look around at each other, thinking.]

Nancy: *[speaking so softly that the kids have to lean in to hear her]* Well, I have an idea. It's—no, it wouldn't work.

Luis: What? What?

Nancy: Well, nobody would have anything like it.

Amanda: What is it?

Nancy: Well, what about Liz? She could rhyme!

Luis: Rhyme?

George: Rhyme?

Nancy: Rhyme!

Amanda: How could rhyming be a talent? And how could we be part of that? Not that we'd ever want to, of course!

Nancy: Easy! Liz is great at making up rhymes. We could have kids call out words and Liz could make up a rhyme about each one! Then we could repeat whatever Liz says—we'd be her backup rhymers!

George: Cool!

Luis: Yeah! Let's do it!

Amanda: You know, I hate to admit it, but that is a good idea. That is, I mean, if Liz will do it after the way I treated her. *[Everyone looks over at Liz.]*

Liz: A rhyming show?
I'm ready to go!

Ms. Jordan: Then let's begin—we have a lot of rhymes to fit in!
*[Everybody laughs at their teacher's attempts
to rhyme.]*

Act 4

*The school auditorium. Ms. Jordan and her class are gathering on
the stage. Other students (including Boy 1, Boy 2, and Girl 1 and
Girl 2) are sitting in the audience.*

Ms. Jordan: And now, a big hand for my class who wishes to present
their most unusual act: Rhymin' Liz and the Rhyme-
Time Kids.

[applause]

Ms. Jordan: Audience, just take turns calling out words and
Rhymin' Liz will make up an instant rhyme about
your word. Then, for your listening pleasure, the
Rhyme-Time Kids will repeat Liz's rhyme. Let's begin
with that boy over there.

Boy 1: Bat!

Liz: That's an easy one, a rhyme for *bat*—
A fat rat sat
on a cat's hat
for a chat!

**Rhyme-Time
Kids:** That's an easy one, a rhyme for *bat*—
A fat rat sat
on a cat's hat
for a chat!

Ms. Jordan: And now you in the front row.

Girl 1: You'll never get this one: strawberry!

Liz: Just my luck, the Dictionary Fairy
granted me a rhyme for the word *strawberry*!

**Rhyme-Time
Kids:** Just my luck, the Dictionary Fairy
granted me a rhyme for the word *strawberry*!

Ms. Jordan: OK! Now you over there!

Boy 2: Try this, rhyming girl: fish stick!

[The audience giggles and snickers.]

Liz: *[taps temple with finger, pretending to be stuck]* Hmmm.
A rhyme for *fish stick*?
Here's the rhyme I pick!

[Liz snaps her fingers.]

**Rhyme-Time
Kids:** A rhyme for *fish stick*?
Here's the rhyme I pick!

[Kids snap their fingers, too.]

Boy 1: She's amazing!

Girl 2: How does she do it?

Boy 2: I don't get it. She seems to have a rhyme for everything!

[Later, at the end of the show . . .]

Boy 1: OK, everyone, it's time to award the prize for the best act. The judges agreed that it was a difficult choice—everyone put on a great act. But they also agreed that the winner of this year's trophy is Rhymin' Liz and the Rhyme-Time Kids!

[Boy 1 hands a trophy to Liz while the rest of Ms. Jordan's class cheers loudly.]

Amanda: Liz, thanks to you we won! I'm sorry I was mean to you.

Liz: That's alright, that's OK!
I don't like to rhyme every day.
Some days I just like to talk in Pig Latin!

Everybody but Liz: *[groaning]* Oh no! Here we go again!

The End

Planting Seeds, Spreading Sunshine
Teaching Notes

Background

Johnny Appleseed was born John Chapman in Leominster, Massachusetts, in 1774. He grew up on a farm with a large apple orchard. At the age of 20, Johnny strapped a bag of apple seeds to his back and headed west to the Ohio Valley. When he arrived, he began a lifelong mission: going from town to town, planting apple trees and sharing seeds with settlers. Johnny, who died in 1845, became a nationally known celebrity when a story about his deeds appeared in an 1871 issue of *Harper's* magazine. Since then, many tales have circulated about him, including claims that he spent a snowy evening snuggled up to a hibernating bear and that he had a knack for communicating with animals. No one can say for certain how true these stories are, but Johnny Appleseed remains one of America's most popular folk heroes.

Extension Activities

Sow Some Tall Tales

In the 19th century, lots of folks passed the time making up stories about Johnny Appleseed. Invite students to do the same now. Begin by discussing Johnny as a folk hero. Point out that while he was a real person, people often told exaggerated tales about his life for entertainment. Brainstorm a list of what-if scenarios with Johnny at the core. For example, what if Johnny befriended a chatty chipmunk or married a woman whose passion was peaches? Divide the class into pairs or groups and challenge them to develop an idea from the list into a tall tale. Publish the stories in a Johnny Appleseed Tall Tale Anthology, complete with illustrations.

Apple Fest

Celebrate Johnny Appleseed's September 26th birthday with a class Apple Fest. Invite students and parents to contribute some of their favorite apple dishes, such as apple bread, apple pie, apple fritters, etc. (Be sure to check for allergies, first.) Label each treat and let students sample. Students might also enjoy making dried-apple-head dolls, or reading aloud stories about Johnny Appleseed. Cap off the festivities by planting apple seeds or taking a field trip to an apple orchard.

Planting Seeds, Spreading Sunshine

by Liza Charlesworth

Characters

- Narrator
- John Chapman
  (Johnny Appleseed)
- Pa
- Ma
- Settlers 1–9
- Nellie Nead

Act 1

A farm in Leominster, Massachusetts, 1794.

Narrator: John Chapman was born in Leominster, Massachusetts, in 1774. He grew up on a farm full of apple trees. Johnny liked to pick the shiny red apples. But even more, he loved to plant apple seeds so that new trees would grow. When Johnny was 20 years old, he decided it was time to go west.

Pa: We're going to miss you around here, son—especially at apple pickin' time. You're the best darn tree climber in the family.

Johnny: I'll miss you, too. But I have to go west to Ohio because there are no apple trees there.

Ma: *[confused]* But I thought you loved apple trees?

Johnny: I do. That's why I'm going. I want to plant seeds so that all the settlers moving there will have wonderful apple trees like ours.

Ma: *[handing Johnny a sack]* Here's some food in case you get hungry. Apple fritters, apple butter, applesauce, and a big slice of apple pie.

Johnny: *[smiling]* Thank you, Ma. They're all my favorites. How did you know?

Ma: *[with a laugh]* Just a lucky guess!

Johnny: *[hugging Ma and Pa]* Good-bye, Ma! Good-bye, Pa! Wish me luck!

Pa: Good-bye, son, and good luck!

Ma: Take care! You'll always be the apple of my eye.

[Johnny waves and walks away.]

Act 2

The woods of Ohio, a few months later.

Narrator: Johnny walked west for many weeks, seeing nothing but trees, flowers, birds, and animals. At last, he met some settlers who were building a log cabin.

Settler 1: Hello there! What brings you to our neck of the woods?

Johnny: I've come all the way from Massachusetts to give you these apple seeds.

Settler 1: *[whispering to Settler 2]* Pssst! Get a load of this guy!

Settler 2: That's . . . er . . . kind of you. But we just moved here from New York and are way too busy to bother with your silly apple seeds.

Johnny: They're not silly! Just plant a seed today, and in a few years you'll have a beautiful apple tree.

Settler 1: So?

Johnny: So! . . . so that means you'll have lots of juicy apples to eat when you're hungry. You'll have a special, shady place to sit when you want to read a good book. And that's not all: You'll be able to climb to the tree's top and wave to your neighbor . . . when you get a neighbor, that is.

Settler 2:   Gee, that does sound pretty good, but we don't have any money to give you for the seeds.

Johnny: That's all right. Just plant a seed and I'll be happy.

Settler 1:   Wow, you're A-OK Mister! Now, what did you say your name was?

Johnny: John Chapman.

Settler 2:   John Chapman . . . would ya' mind if we call you Johnny Appleseed?

Johnny: Not at all. Folks may think it's corny, but I think it's positively . . . apple-y! See you!

Settlers 1 and 2:   *[waving]* Bye!

[Johnny exits.]

Act 3

The woods of Ohio, several years later.

Narrator: Year after year, Johnny walked through the Ohio Valley planting apple seeds and giving apple seeds to everyone he met. By now, many settlers knew about this strange and generous man.

[Johnny crosses paths with some settlers and hands seeds to them as he greets them.]

Johnny: It's an apple of a morning!

Settler 3: Thanks, Johnny!

Johnny: An apple a day, keeps the doctor away.

Settlers 4 and 5: Thank you, Johnny!

Johnny: Cherries are red and berries are, too. But apples are the best for you!

Settler 6: Awesome! Thanks a lot, Johnny!

Johnny: Greetings, young lady. Have some apple seeds to plant.

Nellie Nead: *[in a mocking tone]*
Johnny Appleseed, I've heard of you.
Planting apple seeds is all you do.
Sharing seeds in the sun
and seeds in the rain—
I wouldn't be surprised
if you had an apple for a brain!

Johnny: *[with a laugh]* An apple for a brain . . . I like that!

Nellie: *[in a snobby tone]* And what's with that outfit?
Are you on your way to a costume party?

Johnny: *[examining his clothes]* Well, let's see. I don't spend much time thinking about my duds. But this tin pot here makes a fine hat and it's great for cooking apple dumplings. And this wonderful bag holds lots of apple seeds. Have some! *[tries to put seeds into Nellie's hands]*

Nellie: *[pulling her hands away]* I don't want any dopey seeds. What good are they?

Johnny: If you plant some, you'll find out. All it takes is care and some patience.

Nellie: That's dumb!

Johnny: *[tipping his tin-pot hat]* Suit yourself. Bye.

[After Johnny walks away, Nellie picks up the seeds and puts them in her pocket.]

Act 4

The woods of Ohio, 1840.

Narrator: In 1840, Johnny was 66 years old. But his life hadn't changed very much. He still spent his time planting apple seeds and giving them to settlers. Everyone came to love Johnny . . . even Nellie, who was now a grown woman.

Johnny: Nature's most perfect fruit!

Settler 7:   Thank you, Johnny!

Johnny: Nothing is peachier 'n apples!

Settler 8:   Cool!

Settler 9:   Thanks, Johnny!

Johnny: Hello! Have some apple seeds to plant.

Nellie: Johnny? Johnny Appleseed?

Johnny: That's what they call me. And you are . . . ?

Nellie: You don't remember me?

Johnny: *[looking closely at Nellie's face]* Can't say as I do . . .

Nellie: I'm Nellie Nead. Does this ring a bell?—
Johnny Appleseed, I've heard of you.
Planting apple seeds is all you do.
Sharing seeds in the sun
and seeds in the rain.
I wouldn't be surprised
if you had an apple for a brain!

Johnny: *[laughing]* Oh yes, the odd girl who didn't like apples.

Nellie: That's right. I was pretty bratty back then. Is it too late to say I'm sorry . . . and thank you?

Johnny: *[surprised]* Thank you . . . for what?

Nellie: *[sweeping arm across the edge of a large field of apple trees]* For my beautiful apple orchard. After you walked away, I picked up the seeds and decided to plant them. You were right. All it took was care and patience.

Johnny: I'm APPLE-solutely thrilled!

Nellie: Now . . . how about coming over to my house?
I just baked an apple pie and I want you to be the first to try it.

Johnny: I thought something smelled good! Let's go!

The End

The Hidden Corn
Teaching Notes

Background

Use The Hidden Corn, based on a Mexican folktale, as part of a class recognition of Hispanic Heritage Month, which is celebrated between September 15th and October 15th each year. Hispanic Heritage Month honors the diverse peoples of Spanish-speaking backgrounds who have come to the United States from many countries around the world. It is an opportune time for you and your students to share, discover, and appreciate the contributions and rich heritage of Hispanics in the United States.

This particular play is part of a long-standing tradition of folktales and myth-stories in Mexican culture.

Extension Activities

An Origin-al Idea

The Hidden Corn is an example of an origin story, a tale devised to explain the origin of a certain aspect of life. Share with students some other origin stories from Mexico and other Hispanic cultures. (*Horse Hooves and Chicken Feet: Mexican Folktales* selected by Neil Philip [Clarion, 2002], a collection of 15 retellings, is one excellent resource.) Then let students select one origin story to depict on a mural. Have students make a list of what in the story happened first, second, third, etc. Divide a bulletin board into enough vertical panels to represent each event in the story. Have students fill in each panel with illustrations that retell the story.

Corn Fest

For thousands of years, corn has been a staple in the Mexican diet as well as in those of other Hispanic cultures. Help students learn about this important food by having them research the life cycle of a corn plant, how farmers grow and harvest corn, and ways corn is used in foods and other products (corn oil, cornmeal, corn syrup, packaging materials, ethanol). You might also share books that illustrate the significance of food in Hispanic cultures, such as *The Tortilla Factory* by Gary Paulsen (Voyager Books, 1998), *Growing Up With Tamales* by Gwendolyn Zepeda (Piñata Books, 2008), and *Too Many Tamales* by Gary Soto (Putnam, 1993). Then invite students to collect and share recipes for Hispanic dishes that use corn.

The Hidden Corn

A Folktale of the Mopan People of Mexico

adapted by Deborah Kovacs

Characters

- Narrator
- Ant 1
- Ant 2
- Fox
- Crow
- Skunk
- Coyote
- Boy
- Girl
- Yaluk (Yah-lŏok),
  the Lightning God
- Woodpecker

Act 1

Near a big rock in a forest.

Narrator: Once, long ago, people and animals did not eat corn. They ate fruit that grew on trees and roots that grew under the ground. Nobody had ever seen corn. But there was corn on earth—just one pile of kernels. It was under a rock in a big forest. One day, two ants crawled inside a tiny crack in the big rock. They found the corn.

Ant 1: Hey, this stuff is good!

Ant 2: Let's bring some to our nest.

Narrator: As the ants carried the corn kernels out from under the rock, they dropped one. A fox came along and ate it.

Fox: *[crunching the corn kernel]* That is the most delicious thing I have ever put in my mouth.

Narrator: After that, every day, a whole army of ants came and took corn out from under the rock and took it back to their nest. And every day, the fox was waiting to pick up the kernels they dropped. Once, it started to rain. The ants dropped the kernels they were carrying, and ran for safety.

Fox: A whole pile of corn! Yippee!

SCENE 2

Outside the fox's den.

Narrator: The fox had a feast. He ate so much corn that there was still some on his whiskers when he walked back to his den. Along the way, he ran into a crow, a skunk, and a coyote.

Crow: How's it going, Fox?

Fox: *[still chewing]* Mmm! Good!

Skunk: Say, what are you eating?

Fox: *[still chewing, shaking his head]* Oh, nothing.

Coyote: What's that on your whisker? *[flicks corn off Fox's whiskers]* Is this food? *[tastes it]* Say, that's mighty good! Where did you find it?

Fox: Oh, nowhere!

SCENE 3

Back at the rock.

Narrator: The other animals were suspicious. They followed Fox the next day and discovered his secret.

Coyote: So that's what he's up to.

Skunk: How do we get some?

Crow: Let's ask the ants for help.

Narrator: The ants did what they could. Again and again they went into the crack, bringing out corn. Finally, they were worn out. The other animals wanted too much corn.

Ant 1: We can't help you any more.

Ant 2: Sorry.

Skunk: Let's try to squeeze into the crack. *[tries and fails]*

Coyote: That's ridiculous!

Crow: Now what do we do?

Fox: Everything was okay until you guys butted in . . .

Act 2

SCENE 1

In a village.

Narrator: The animals asked a boy and a girl for help.

Boy: There's not much I can do. Wait! I have an idea: I'll ask Yaluk, the Lightning God, for help.

Girl: Yaluk could send down a bolt of lightning to break the rock.

SCENE 2

On a hill, above the village, overlooking the big rock.

Narrator: The children called to Yaluk for help.

Boy and Girl: Yaluk! Please send down a lightning bolt to split this rock. We want to get the corn hidden inside.

Yaluk: Break a rock? That's a piece of cake. Fetch me a woodpecker, first.

SCENE 3

In the forest.

Narrator: The boy and the girl searched the forest until they found a woodpecker.

Girl: Yaluk needs your help, Woodpecker!

Boy: Will you come with us?

Woodpecker: Yaluk? You mean the Yaluk? The Lightning God? Wow! You bet!

SCENE 4

Outside the fox's den.

Yaluk: I want you to tap everywhere on that rock until you find the thinnest place.

Woodpecker: Yes sir, Mr. Yaluk, sir! Right away! *[Woodpecker taps.]* Here's the spot you want!

Yaluk: Now stay back while I throw down this lightning bolt.

Narrator: The woodpecker tried to stay out of the way, but his curiosity got the better of him.

Woodpecker: I wonder what it looks like . . .

Narrator: The lightning bounced off the woodpecker's head.

Woodpecker: OUCH!

Boy: Are you all right?

Woodpecker: [dazed] I . . . I think so.

Girl: Your head feathers are all red!

Narrator: Yaluk split the rock open, and the boy and the girl took out corn to plant for their families and to share with all the animals who wanted some. From that day to this, people and animals have eaten corn . . . [Woodpecker wanders by, dazed.] . . . And woodpeckers have always had red heads . . . [to Woodpecker] Say, are you all right?

Woodpecker: I . . . I think so . . . .

The End

The Ugly Pumpkin
Teaching Notes

Background

Share with students these interesting facts about pumpkins:

- Pumpkins are fruits in the squash family. Other types of squash include acorn, banana, butternut, hubbard, spaghetti, and zucchini.
- From seed to mature fruit, pumpkins take about four months to grow.
- Most pumpkins weigh between 15 and 30 pounds, but some record holders have weighed as much as 1,500 pounds!
- Pumpkins are a good source of vitamin A and potassium. Their seeds are rich in protein and iron.
- People around the world cook pumpkins and other squashes in many different ways—boiled, baked, steamed, or roasted. They are also used in breads, soups, and of course, pies.
- Pumpkin pie, so popular in the United States, is said to have originated with early American colonists. They would poke a hole in the top of a pumpkin (or cut off the top), scoop out the seeds, and then fill the hollow pumpkin with milk, spices, and honey. They then baked the pumpkin in the hot ashes that remained from a fire.

Extension Activities

Pumpkin Research

Visit a local pumpkin farm. Before the trip, generate a list of interview questions to pose to the pumpkin farmers. For example, ask farmers to describe a pumpkin's life cycle from seed to fruit, as well as what weather factors affect pumpkin growth. Ask them to describe the harvest: how it is done and how long the harvest season lasts. Ask them to show examples of pumpkin varieties. Students might also find out which pumpkin types grow the largest. And finally, which pumpkins make the best pumpkin pie?

Pumpkin Poem

Write the following categories on the board: *See, Hear, Feel, Smell.* Pass a pumpkin among the students. Have them dictate words describing the pumpkin according to each sensory category. Record their contributions under each heading. Cut the pumpkin open and repeat the activity. If the class made a pumpkin pie or roasted pumpkin seeds as part of another activity, add *taste* to the list of categories. Post the list in your writing corner and suggest students refer to the list when writing pumpkin stories and poems.

The Ugly Pumpkin

by Carol Pugliano-Martin

Characters

- Farmer Smith
- Farmer Jones
- Priscilla Pumpkin
- Peter Pumpkin
- Peggy Pumpkin
- Patrick Pumpkin
- Patty Pumpkin
- Paul Pumpkin
- Ugly Pumpkin
- Matthew
- Lauren
- Eric
- Olivia
- Teacher

Act 1

A pumpkin patch. All the sprouts look the same, except for the Ugly Pumpkin, who is a bit off to himself. Farmer Smith and Farmer Jones enter.

Farmer Smith: The pumpkin sprouts are coming up very nicely this year!

Farmer Jones: Yes, they are. I was worried that we did not have enough rain this spring to help them to grow.

Farmer Smith: Well, I don't think you have to worry anymore. I am sure we will sell all the pumpkins this year!

Farmer Jones: I hope so. The school is having a jack-o-lantern contest, and I want to have plenty of good pumpkins for the children to choose from!

Farmer Smith: They will with this crop! *[Farmer Smith stops at the Ugly Pumpkin.]* Hey, this sprout looks a bit odd, don't you think?

Farmer Jones: You're right. Oh, and I really thought the whole crop was doing so well.

Farmer Smith: Well, let's not worry too much right now. It is too early. Let's wait until growing season and then we'll see.

Farmer Jones: That's right. No sense in jinxing the crop with bad thoughts! Hey, how about some breakfast?

Farmer Smith: You are always thinking about food! Come on inside. I'll make some pumpkin pancakes.

[They exit.]

Act 2

The pumpkin patch, a few months later.

Priscilla Pumpkin: Hey! Look at me! Look at me! I'm a pumpkin! Priscilla Pumpkin!

Peter Pumpkin: We're all pumpkins, silly! I'm Peter.

Peggy Pumpkin: My name is Peggy. You *must* look at my beautiful orange color!

Patrick Pumpkin: Look at how round I am! My name is Patrick.

Patty Pumpkin: I'm Patty and I am a perfect circle!

Paul Pumpkin: I'm Paul, the biggest one here!

[All of the pumpkins turn to look at the Ugly Pumpkin.]

Priscilla Pumpkin: Hey, what's up with that one?

Peter Pumpkin: Yeah. He looks weird!

Peggy Pumpkin: He's shaped like a bell or something!

Patrick Pumpkin: And he's a strange light-yellow color!

Patty Pumpkin: What is he doing here with us? What kind of a pumpkin is he?

Paul Pumpkin: I'll find out. Hey, you! What are you, anyway? You are the strangest looking pumpkin we have ever seen!

Ugly Pumpkin: Uhh . . . My name is Samuel.

Paul Pumpkin: Samuel? Even your name is different!

Ugly Pumpkin: I know, I know. I wish I were more like all of you! I'm . . . I'm so ugly!

[He bows his head and starts crying.]

Priscilla Pumpkin: There, there. Don't cry.

Peter Pumpkin: Yeah. Take it easy.

Peggy Pumpkin: You're not so bad.

Patrick Pumpkin: Just a little different, that's all.

Ugly Pumpkin: None of the children will pick me for the contest!

Patty Pumpkin: Shh. I hear voices. It's the children! Everybody look your best!

[Matthew, Lauren, Eric, and Olivia enter and walk among the pumpkins.]

Matthew: What a great pumpkin patch!

Lauren: There are so many pumpkins!

Eric: I'll never be able to choose!

Matthew: Hmmm . . . Let's see. I think I'll take this one.

[He picks up Priscilla Pumpkin and walks off.]

Lauren: This one looks perfect for me!

[She takes Peter Pumpkin and exits.]

Eric: This one's mine!

[He takes Peggy Pumpkin and exits. One by one, other children take Patty Pumpkin, Paul Pumpkin, and Patrick Pumpkin, leaving only Olivia and the Ugly Pumpkin.]

Olivia: *[looking around to see if there are any other pumpkins left]* I guess I'll take this one.

[The Ugly Pumpkin beams as they start to exit. Matthew enters.]

Matthew: Did you pick your pumpkin?

Olivia: Yes. Here it is.

Matthew: Are you joking? That's the weirdest looking pumpkin I've ever seen! You'll never win the contest with that one!

[He laughs and runs off.]

Olivia: Oh, I think it's kind of cute. Come on, pumpkin. I'll carve a great face on you, and we'll just see who wins!

[They exit.]

ACT 3

In the classroom.

Teacher: Come on, children. Line up your jack-o-lanterns so we can begin the judging.

[All the children enter with their pumpkins. Olivia and the Ugly Pumpkin are last.]

Teacher: *[walking down the line]* Hmmm . . . very nice. Oh, cute! Interesting! Oooo! Scary! *[stops at the Ugly Pumpkin]* Well, well. What have we here?

Matthew: That's Olivia's pumpkin. *[He laughs.]*

Teacher: Well that's not a pumpkin at all. It's a butternut squash! And an adorable one at that!

Kids and Pumpkins together: A BUTTERNUT SQUASH!

Teacher: Of course! The farmer must have planted it in the pumpkin patch by mistake. Well, Olivia, it looks like you have the most unique entry of all. You win!

Lauren: She does? But why?

Teacher: I have never seen a squash-o-lantern before. That was very clever of you, Olivia!

Olivia: Uh . . . Thank you!

Eric: Come on. Let's go home and make our pies for the pumpkin pie contest. There's no way she can win that!

Matthew: Well, I wouldn't be so sure.

The End

A Native American Welcome
Teaching Notes

Background

When the Mayflower left England in 1620, it carried the hopes of its 102 passengers. Some of them had left to make their fortune in what they called the New World, while the others had broken away from the Church of England and wanted to worship as they pleased. The trip was extremely difficult: One person died and many were sick. The passengers agreed to begin their life in North America together and signed the *Mayflower Compact*, which described how they would govern themselves.

Once on the Massachusetts shore, life was no easier. The winter was harsh; by its end, less than half of the Pilgrims were alive, felled by disease and starvation. That spring, Samoset, a leader of the Abenaki peoples, and Squanto, a Wampanoag, encountered the Pilgrims and offered them their help. Squanto's own village had been wiped out by disease, so he stayed with the Pilgrims and became an indispensable friend and teacher. Without his help, the Pilgrims would not have survived. The following autumn, Squanto, together with Massasoit (the Wampanoag chief), his wife, and 90 Wampanoag men, attended the Pilgrims' first Thanksgiving.

Extension Activities

Giving Thanks Around the Year

The Wampanoag celebrated many "Thanksgivings" long before the arrival of the Pilgrims in 1620. At these seasonal harvest festivals, still celebrated throughout the year, the Wampanoag express their gratitude for the gifts of the land. In July, for example, they celebrate a Green Corn Thanksgiving (green corn is immature, but edible and sweet). In October they have a Cranberry Thanksgiving.

Give each student a sheet of copy paper. Tell students to fold it in half and then write the name of one of the four seasons at the top of each half-page. Encourage students to think of gifts from nature that they are thankful for each season, such as the warm, summer sun or a beautiful snowfall in winter. Students can then write and illustrate things they are grateful for on the page for each season.

The Way to North America

The trip on the *Mayflower* was adventurous—and a huge risk for the passengers. Have students trace the trip, from its launching on September 6, 1620 in Plymouth, England, to the first sighting of land on November 11 at what is now known as Cape Cod, Massachusetts. Help students trace the route on a map, figure out how long the trip was, or even how many miles the ship went on an average day. You might want to discuss how long such a trip would take to complete today.

A Native American Welcome

by Sandra Widener

Characters

- Narrator
- Wampanoag 1
  (WAHM-puh-NOH-ahg)
- Wampanoag 2
- Squanto
- Samoset
- Edward Winslow
- Elizabeth Hopkins
- Massasoit
- Sarah Hopkins

Act 1

Plymouth, Massachusetts; Spring, 1621.

Narrator: The Pilgrims left England and sailed to North America in 1620 because they wanted to start a new life. That first winter, though, they almost starved. During those months, the Native Americans who already lived in the area were curious about the newcomers.

[The Pilgrims are shivering and planting wheat kernels by tossing them on the ground. The Native Americans watching the Pilgrims from behind trees.]

Wampanoag 1: They look cold.

Wampanoag 2: They look hungry, too. Have you watched them plant? Their seeds will never grow.

Wampanoag 1: Should we try to help them? What if they try to attack us?

Squanto: I know the English. They will not hurt us. Men who attack never bring families. If we don't help them, they will have trouble getting through the rough winter when food is scarce.

Samoset: I agree. I learned their language from other ship captains. Let's talk to them.

[Samoset and the other Native Americans walk around the trees to greet the Pilgrims, who step back in surprise and fear.]

Edward Winslow: Who—who are you?

Samoset: *[extending his hand]* Welcome.

Edward Winslow: *[shaking Samoset's hand in amazement]* You speak our language!

Samoset: Yes.

Edward Winslow: *[with a small laugh]* Well, welcome!

Squanto: We are afraid for you. Conditions are harsh here. I will stay and teach you how to plant corn. I can show you how to catch fish, and which berries to eat.

Elizabeth Hopkins: *[with a frown]* Why would you do that for us?

Squanto: I do not want to see you starve. I can stay with you because I have no tribe.

Elizabeth Hopkins: *[smiling at him]* I think you are the luck we have been seeking in this new land.

Act 2

A Wampanoag settlement not far from Plymouth Colony, November 1621.

[Squanto walks up to the other Native Americans.]

Samoset: Squanto! Where have you been?

Squanto: With the settlers. They really needed help! I taught them to plant corn with fish heads, the way we do it. Then I showed them how to get maple syrup from the trees, and which plants to eat.

Wampanoag 1:	Their ways are strange.
Squanto:	Yes, they are different from us. But they are good people.
Wampanoag 2:	I still don't trust them. Other settlers have hurt our people.
Squanto:	Not these settlers. They appreciate my help. In fact, they are planning a feast to celebrate their harvest. Let's join them.
Samoset:	A feast like our Cranberry festival?
Squanto:	I don't know what they call it, but it is a harvest festival like our Cranberry festival.
Wampanoag 1:	I'll trust you, Squanto. Let's go!
Wampanoag 2:	I'll go, too! And I know some others who would like to come.

Act 3

The Plymouth settlement, November, 1621. Pilgrim women and children are preparing dinner.

Elizabeth Hopkins:	Quick, children! Bring the cornbread here! Carry that fruit to the table!

[Sarah Hopkins and the other children carry items to the table and then go stand near their mothers.]

Edward Winslow: Well, Mistress Hopkins, it will be a fine feast. I see little Sarah here is helping, too. *[He bends to pat Sarah on the head, then straightens again.]*

Sarah Hopkins: *[tugging harder at Elizabeth Hopkins's skirt]* Mother, over there! Look who's coming!

[Elizabeth Hopkins and Edward Winslow turn to see a line of Native Americans walking toward them.]

Elizabeth Hopkins: *[gasping]* There must be 90 of them! What shall we feed them? If we feed them all, we will have no food for winter!

[Squanto and the other Native Americans walk up to Elizabeth Hopkins and Edward Winslow.]

Squanto: I have brought the chief of the tribe.

Edward Winslow: Welcome. Without the help of Squanto, we would not be alive now.

Massasoit: Thank you. *[looking at the food on the table]* But I see that you were not prepared for so much help eating your feast! There is not enough to go around.

[Edward Winslow and Elizabeth Hopkins look at each other.]

Elizabeth Hopkins: We will gladly share what we have.

Massasoit: That will not be necessary. *[He nods at the Wampanoag group.]* They will return with more food.

[The tribe members leave.]

Sarah Hopkins: *[tugging on her mother's skirt again]* Hey, Mother, when can we eat?

[Everyone laughs.]

Elizabeth Hopkins: She's right. Help yourselves, everyone! We'll make do with what we have.

[The Wampanoag tribe members return, carrying deer.]

Wampanoag 1: We bring you deer meat.

Edward Winslow: This is a fine gift! You will always be welcome here with us.

Elizabeth Hopkins: We know that without you, there would be no feast—and no harvest.

Sarah Hopkins: *[her mouth full as she eats an apple]* No harvest! No food! That's terrible!

[Everyone laughs.]

Elizabeth Hopkins: Let us hope this is the beginning of a long friendship. Happy Thanksgiving, everyone!

The End

The Hesitant Hibernator
Teaching Notes

Background

Bears usually settle in their dens before the first snowfall and hibernate for the coldest months of the year, December through March. When hibernating, bears do not fall into a very deep sleep the way woodchucks and other hibernating animals do. They can be disturbed and can wake up to protect themselves. Sometimes they come out of their dens for a while during a warm spell.

The most amazing thing about bear hibernation is the way a bear's metabolism changes. A hibernating bear does not eat, drink or eliminate waste, yet it does not become dehydrated or lose body weight or muscle. This is because the bear's body is able to recycle waste products to maintain muscle tissue and keep the water content of its body in balance.

Extension Activities

Who Hibernates?
Help students find out more about hibernation by having them research the different types of hibernation, how it differs from sleep, and what animals hibernate. They can also find out places animals hibernate (such as caves, dens, burrows) and how they prepare for their winter's nap (for example, eating lots of food to increase body fat).

Have students create a list of animals that hibernate and put them into categories: those that are true hibernators or "super hibernators," those that go into a state of dormancy or diapause, and others that go into a daily state of torpor. Your lesson might also include other ways animals deal with wintertime, for example, by migrating.

The Wide World of Bears
Share this poem with your students:

Bear, bear, bear, bear!
How many kinds of bears are there?
Polar bear and grizzly bear,
Big brown bear with lots of hair!
Spectacled bear, black bear too,
Sloth bear, sun bear, quite a few!
Bear, bear, bear, bear!
So many bears to compare.

—by Meish Goldish

After you've read the poem, invite groups of students to research and prepare fact books on one of the types of bears mentioned in the rhyme. When the groups have finished, let them share what they've learned with the class. Add the books to your class library for students to enjoy throughout the year.

The Hesitant Hibernator

by Cass Hollander

Characters

- Narrator
- Twin Bear 1
- Twin Bear 2
- Snowshoe Hare
- Groundhog 1
- Groundhog 2

Act 1

The woods in October.

Narrator: Mother bears give birth to their cubs usually between January and March, even during hibernation. The cubs stay with their mother for about two years, and then set out on their own. This story is about twin bears on their own for the first time. In June, they say good-bye to their mother and spend the summer fishing, eating berries, and climbing trees. As our story opens, it's October.

Twin Bear 1: Isn't the world amazing? The leaves were green. Then they turned yellow, orange, and red. Now they're falling off the trees—

Twin Bear 2: So are the acorns! *[scoops up acorns with both paws and gobbles them up]* Yum!

Twin Bear 1: Stop eating! You're getting fat! You're huge!

Twin Bear 2: I'm a bear! I'm supposed to be huge! *[tearing into a decaying log]* Wow! Look at all these bugs in this old rotten log! *[scooping up bugs and eating them by the pawful]* Delicious! Here. Try some. *[offers the other bear a pawful of bugs]*

Twin Bear 1: No, thanks. I'm not hungry.

Twin Bear 2: *[still gobbling bugs]* You better get hungry! If you don't eat, you're gonna wake up starving halfway through winter. You won't be able to hibernate all winter long.

Twin Bear 1: I've decided not to hibernate this year.

Twin Bear 2: *[nearly chokes with surprise]* What? Not hibernate? You have to hibernate. You're a bear. It's what bears do.

Twin Bear 1: Haven't you ever wondered what happens in the winter? Aren't you curious?

Twin Bear 2: About winter? No. Let's see if there are any nuts under that tree.

Twin Bear 1: Well, I'm curious. I don't want to sleep for four months. That's one third of the whole year. Why should I spend one third of the year asleep?

Twin Bear 2: Because you're a bear. It's what bears do.

Twin Bear 1: Not this bear!

Act 2

The woods in late December.

Narrator: When the last autumn leaf finally fell, and when white flakes began to fall in soft mounds over all the woodlands, one of our bear friends knew it was time to snuggle deep in a dark, cozy cave and settle down to sleep. But our other bear friend decided to stay awake to see what winter was really like.

Twin Bear 1: *[He runs around in a circle, then rolls on his back in the snow.]* This stuff is great! It's fluffy. It's fun to roll in. I wonder what it is. Look at these things hanging from the tree. *[breaking an icicle off a fir tree]* Pretty amazing. *[puts icicle in mouth]* Hmmm. Tastes like cold water. I wonder what you call this? *[looks around and moves one hind paw around in the snow]* Winter's nice. But where is everybody?

[Snowshoe Hare hops over. She sees the bear and starts to hop away fast.]

Twin Bear 1: Wait!

Snowshoe Hare: Are you kidding! I'm not going to be your bedtime snack! *[The hare hops on one foot then the other to keep warm.]*

Twin Bear 1: What are you talking about? I don't want to eat you! I'm not even hungry!

Snowshoe Hare: Then what are you doing up? My mama told me the only reason bears wake up in winter is because they didn't eat enough before they went to sleep. So they get up to find a snack. And I'm *not* gonna be *your* snack!

Twin Bear 1: I didn't get up to find a snack. I didn't get up at all! I'm not hibernating.

Snowshoe Hare: Not hibernating? Why not? You're a bear.

Twin Bear 1: I didn't want to miss winter.

Snowshoe Hare: What's to miss? It gets cold. The water freezes. There's nothing to eat but bark. I hate it. I'd hibernate if I could. *[The hare turns to go.]*

Twin Bear 1: Wait! You're the first living thing I've seen in days. Where is everybody?

**Snowshoe
  Hare:** Well, some animals are hibernating—like you should be. The birds migrated to someplace warm. And the rest of us try to stay out of the cold as much as we can. *[The hare starts to hop away.]*

Twin Bear 1: Wait! Stay and talk with me.

**Snowshoe
  Hare:** I'm cold. I hate hopping around in the snow. I'm going home where it's warm.

[The bear looks a little forlorn watching the hare hop away.]

Act 3

The woods in February. In a groundhog hole, two groundhogs are asleep inside. The bear is sitting on a stump near the groundhog hole, looking bored.

Narrator: It's the second day of February. Winter has dragged on for two long, cold months. All that time the ground has been covered with snow.

Twin Bear 1: The worst thing about winter is that nothing happens. There's nothing to do. Nobody's around. *[He holds chin in paw and stares off into space.]*

[Groundhogs start to stir in their hole.]

Groundhog 1: *[stretching]* I think I'll take a little walk outside. See what's happening.

Groundhog 2:   *[yawning]* I'm right behind you. *[Groundhog rolls over and goes back to sleep.]*

[Groundhog 1 goes out and sees the bear sitting on the stump. Groundhog 1 screams and runs back into the hole. Inside the hole, Groundhog 2 wakes with a start when it hears the scream.]

Groundhog 2:   What's the matter? Did you see your shadow?

Groundhog 1:   *[frightened]* No. There's a bear right outside our hole!

Groundhog 2:   What's a bear doing up?

Groundhog 1:   It must be hungry.

Groundhog 2:   *[worried]* Don't go out there again. Let's just go back to sleep. We don't have to get up for another six weeks.

[Twin Bear 2 enters and goes over to Twin Bear 1 on stump.]

Twin Bear 2:   Is that you?

Twin Bear 1:   *[jumps up and embraces twin]* I'm so glad to see you! Is it spring?

Twin Bear 2:   I don't think so. I heard some animal scream. It woke me up. I decided to come out and see what was going on. So, how's it going? Are you enjoying winter?

Twin Bear 1:   Not really. I liked the snow . . . at first. But now it's pretty boring. Nothing happens. There's nothing to do. Nobody's around.

Twin Bear 2:   Are you ready to hibernate? You've probably got six weeks before winter's over.

Twin Bear 1:   I don't think I can take six more weeks of winter.

Twin Bear 2:   So, don't. Sleep—the way you're supposed to. Come on. You can share my cave.

Twin Bear 1:   OK. *[yawning]* Next year, I think I'll skip winter.

Twin Bear 2:   Good idea. You could hibernate the winter away. It's what we bears do best!

The End

The Mystery of the Missing Munchies
Teaching Notes

Background

December is a month rich with celebrations. Christmas, Chanukah, and Kwanzaa are just a few of the holidays students' families may be enjoying. Whatever your celebration needs, this play can be customized to reflect your students' particular customs and cultures. You can easily modify portions of the dialogue to reflect your own celebrations. You can also take the experience a step further and have parents or students bake the holiday treats mentioned in the play. Why not use this play as a segue into your own class multicultural fest, with the entire audience joining the cast and the other students for an ethnic celebration?

Extension Activities

Reporting the Story

Tell students to imagine they are in Mr. Kramer's class and have just had their holiday mystery party. What would they write about it for a school newspaper? How would they describe the events? Have students illustrate their stories if they wish. (Hint: To guide their reporting efforts, encourage students to study the journalistic structure found in most newspaper features.)

Family Recipe Magic

Invite students to ask family members to provide copies of favorite family or ethnic recipes to contribute to a Family Recipe Book. Have students copy the recipes onto lined paper. Provide blank pages for students to illustrate with pictures or to add photos of their families eating the recipes featured. Help students develop captions for their illustrations and photos. Bind the pages together into a book and circulate among students and their families.

Add a Little Music

When planning a holiday party, include not only ethnic treats but ethnic music, as well! Ask parents and students to bring instruments or recordings to the festivities so they may share holiday songs and music from their individual cultures or backgrounds. Invite participants to tell why the music is special in their family history or to them personally.

The Mystery of the Missing Munchies

by Sandra Widener

Characters

- Rachel
- Maria
- Denny
- Melody
- Ray
- Mr. Kramer
- Parents

Act 1

Mr. Kramer's classroom, mid-December.

Rachel: Hey, Maria, what are you bringing to the holiday party? I hear there are going to be some tasty munchies for our party.

Maria: *[looking into a bag and taking a sniff]* Rosquillas (ros-KEE-yas). They are my family's favorite. Every year at Christmas we make them.

Rachel: *[looking in bag, too]* What are they?

Maria: They're Spanish doughnuts, the best doughnuts you've ever had!

Denny: *[holding out a casserole]* Look at this! My mom made bastela (bs-TEE-yah). It's from Morocco, and it has almonds and custard.

Melody: *[showing a plate of cookies]* These are sand tarts. My dad says his grandmother ate them when she was a little girl in Sweden.

Rachel: *[showing her plate]*, Well, these are rugelach (RUG-uh-lukh), and my mom helped me make them. They are little pastries that have raisins on the inside. We like to eat them at Chanukah. Are they ever good!

Ray: *[holding a plate]* This is flan. It's a kind of pudding made with milk and eggs and sugar. The recipe comes from my grandparents in the Philippines.

Mr. Kramer: *[walks into the room and looks around]* Mmmm! Those treats smell delicious! We have to go to lunch now, but we'll all save room for our holiday munchies this afternoon. Please put them on the table over there.

Act 2

The classroom, after lunch on the same day.

Ray: *[comes over to the table and sees it is bare except for a folded piece of paper]* Oh no! Rachel! Denny! Maria! Melody! Come quick! They're GONE!

Rachel: What's gone?

Denny: Can't you see? The treats for our holiday party! They're gone! They've been stolen!

Melody: *[looking around]* No party? No cookies? No nothing? I'm going to cry.

Maria: That won't do any good. *[She leans over and looks at the paper on the table.]* Wait. What's this? *[Maria reads the paper.]* You won't believe this! Whoever took our treats left this note!

Denny: What does it say?

[The children crowd around Maria and the note.]

Maria: It says, "Where the land is green and the water shines blue, you'll find another mystery clue."

Ray: This is making me mad. I just want to eat.

Maria: You can eat as soon as we solve the riddle. Do you have any ideas?

[The children think for a few seconds.]

Melody: I know! Could it be a book about the world? *[She runs to the bookshelf and looks.]* No treats here.

Rachel: Where the water shines blue? Hmmm . . .

Maria: Wait a minute! I know! The globe!

[All the children rush to the globe.]

Melody: I sure don't see any treats here.

Ray: Let's look underneath.

[They lift the globe. Underneath is another note, which Ray holds up and reads.]

Ray: This one says, "Don't be in the dark. You're all so bright. Just walk over and shed some light." What do you think that means?

Maria: Something to do with light. The window? *[She runs over and looks at the glass.]* Nothing there.

Denny: Hey . . . I bet it's the light switch!

[The children rush to the light switch and find another note. Everyone groans. Denny takes the note down.]

Ray: I still just want to eat.

Rachel: Well, what does this note say?

Denny: This one says, "I can hold more words than you've ever seen. But with one wipe, I come clean."

Ray: I don't want to solve riddles. I want to eat!

Melody: We know, we know. But we can't eat until we find out where the food is, can we?

Ray: OK, then, I'll solve it. "Hold more words."Hmmm . . . a computer?

Rachel: Somebody's mind?

Maria: No! But, maybe instead of "hold" more words, the poem means "write" more words. What do you write with?

Ray: Pencils, pens . . .

Denny: It has to be something you can get rid of with one wipe.

Ray and Maria: Chalk!

[They rush to the chalkboard. There is another note. Denny takes it.]

Maria: OK, what does this one say?

Rachel: It says, "Keep moving forward! Go to the place where treats are stored!"

Ray: That's easy. Treats belong in my stomach.

Melody: It must be the lunchroom. Come on, everyone!

[The children walk quickly to the lunchroom. Mr. Kramer and children's parents are there, as well as the pile of treats on a table.]

Mr. Kramer and the Parents:	Surprise!
Maria:	Momma! Poppa! What are you doing here! *[Maria and her parents hug.]*
Maria's Mother:	Mr. Kramer called and told us he was having a big surprise holiday party for all of the children and their parents.
Maria:	It sure is a surprise! Thanks, Mr. Kramer.
Mr. Kramer:	Everyone was going to bring such wonderful things, I thought it would be fun to share. Look—we have treats from all over the world!
Rachel:	Well, you sure surprised us. Good job! And, by the way, good clues, too.
Ray:	OK, OK! Now can we eat?
Mr. Kramer:	Of course. Everyone take a plate! Enjoy the munchies! And happy holidays!

The End

Kindness, the Magic Peacekeeper
Teaching Notes

Background

Chinese New Year is considered the most important of the Chinese holidays. It usually falls somewhere between the middle of January and the middle of February. Celebrated for more than five thousand years, it marks the end of winter and beginning of spring. One month before the end of the old year, families begin preparing for the New Year by cleaning their homes from top to bottom. Much food is prepared in advance as stores and markets will be closed during the New Year festivities. The Chinese New Year celebration lasts for five days. These days are filled with feasting, visiting, and parades.

Extension Activity

The Chinese Zodiac

The Chinese Zodiac is a twelve-year cycle. Each year is named for an animal. Each person has an animal sign representing the year of his or her birth. Many Chinese believe that this animal sign determines one's personality. To see if this is true for your students and their friends and families, copy the information below onto a bulletin board. Use labeled index cards to match the names of students, friends, and family members with the character descriptions of the Chinese Zodiac animals for their birth year. Have students write essays telling why they believe their Zodiac descriptions are accurate or not.

Year of the Pig

1911, 1923, 1935, 1947, 1959, 1971, 1983, 1995, 2007, 2019, etc.

People born in this year are very friendly and loyal. They are also hardworking, honest, and brave.

Year of the Ram

1919, 1931, 1943, 1955, 1967, 1979, 1991, 2003, 2015, etc.

People born in this year are very artistic. They are also generous and understanding, and sometimes shy.

(continues)

Year of the Rabbit

1915, 1927, 1939, 1951, 1963, 1975, 1987, 1999, 2011, etc.

People born in this year tend to be quiet and calm. They like to take care of others. They also pay attention to details.

Year of the Monkey

1920, 1932, 1944, 1956, 1968, 1980, 1992, 2004, 2016, etc.

Monkey people are very clever and have good memories. They are also very good at solving problems.

Year of the Snake

1917, 1929, 1941, 1953, 1965, 1977, 1989, 2001, 2013, etc.

People born in this year love good books, food, music, and plays. They will have good luck with money.

Year of the Rooster

1921, 1933, 1945, 1957, 1969, 1981, 1993, 2005, 2017, etc.

People born in this year are hard workers. They have many talents, like to stay busy, and think deep thoughts.

Year of the Dragon

1916, 1928, 1940, 1952, 1964, 1976, 1988, 2000, 2012, etc.

Dragon people have good health. They like to get things done, and often like to be alone.

Year of the Rat

1912, 1924, 1936, 1948, 1960, 1972, 1984, 1996, 2008, etc.

Rat people are very curious. They like to invent things and are full of energy.

Year of the Ox

1913, 1925, 1937, 1949, 1961, 1973, 1985, 1997, 2009, etc.

People born in this year are very dependable and calm. They are good listeners and have very strong ideas.

Year of the Horse

1918, 1930, 1942, 1954, 1966, 1978, 1990, 2002, 2014, etc.

People born in this year are popular, cheerful, and like to make people laugh.

Year of the Tiger

1914, 1926, 1938, 1950, 1962, 1974, 1986, 1998, 2010, etc.

Tiger people are brave. People respect tiger people for their deep thoughts and courageous actions.

Year of the Dog

1910, 1922, 1934, 1946, 1958, 1970, 1982, 1994, 2006, 2018, etc.

Dog people are loyal and can always keep a secret. They like things to be neat and organized.

Kindness, the Magic Peacekeeper

by Carol Pugliano-Martin

Characters

- Christine
- Kevin
- Grandfather
- Tsao (sow) Wang
- Bao-Yu (bow-yoo) Wang
- Child 1
- Child 2
- Child 3
- Emperor

Act 1

[Grandfather is sitting in a rocking chair. Kevin enters hurriedly, with Christine following.]

Christine: Kevin! Give that dumpling back. It's mine!

Kevin: It is not! Mom gave this to me.

Christine: That's your second one. I saw you sneak it into your pocket after you already ate one.

Kevin: I got an extra one for helping Mom. *[He looks in his hand.]* Oooh, and it looks sooo good!

Christine: Give it to me!

[The two children begin having a tug-of-war with the dumpling. Grandfather enters.]

Grandfather: Now, now. What's going on here?

Christine: Kevin stole my dumpling.

Kevin: I did not! It's mine!

Christine: It isn't. You are a thief!

Kevin: You are a liar!

Grandfather: Children, you must stop this bickering! After all, tonight is New Year's Eve.

Christine: We know, Grandfather—That's why Mom has been cooking all this great food all week.

Kevin: And she gave *me* this dumpling.

Christine: It's *my* dumpling!

Grandfather: You two should not fight tonight. The New Year must begin with peace, joy, and kindness. In fact, you should be kind to each other all year long. Remember Tsao Wang and his family?

Christine: I remember, Grandfather: They were the happiest family ever.

Kevin: I don't remember that.

Christine: You were probably in the kitchen taking food when Grandfather told us that story last year!

Kevin: Was not!

Christine: Were too!

Grandfather: Now, now! I would be happy to tell the story again, when you are ready to listen quietly.

Christine: Yes, Grandfather.

Kevin: OK. We're ready now.

Grandfather: Very well, then. A long, long time ago, there was a man named Tsao Wang.

[Tsao enters.]

He had a very large family and many dogs. They were very happy.

[Tsao Wang's wife, Bao-Yu, enters.]

Tsao: Dinner smells wonderful!

Bao-Yu: It is all ready. I will get the children.

Tsao: No. You sit down and relax. I will get them.

Bao-Yu: Thank you.

Tsao: Children! Dinner is ready.

[The children enter and sit.]

Child 1: Yum! That smells great!

Child 2: It sure does!

Child 3: I can't wait to taste it!

Bao-Yu: Where are the dogs? They must eat, too.

[Child 1 whistles. The dogs run in. They all gather at a dinner table on the floor. Bao-Yu begins serving.]

Bao-Yu: Here you go, dear. And you, my child, and you, and you. And I can't forget our wonderful dogs!

[She serves the dogs, but accidentally leaves one out. That dog hangs its head.]

Child 1: I have more than my [brother/sister]. I will share mine with [him/her].

Tsao: That is very kind of you. But why aren't the dogs eating?

Bao-Yu: Oh my, I forgot to give one of them its meal. Here you go.

[Now all the dogs and people begin eating. Just then, there is a knock at the door.]

Tsao: I will get it.

Child 3:   No, father. I will see who it is. You enjoy your meal.

[He goes to door. The Emperor enters.]

Child 3:   It is the Emperor!

[All stand and bow.]

Tsao: Your majesty. We are honored to have you visit our home.

Emperor: Tsao Wang, I have heard many stories about your family. So many live here in peace. Tell me, what is your secret?

Tsao: It is really very simple.

Emperor: Would you please write it down so that others can live as happily as you do?

Tsao: Of course.

[He gets a piece of paper and writes for a while.]

Tsao: *[handing the Emperor the paper]* Here it is.

Emperor: Thank you. *[He looks at the paper.]* But you have only written one word over and over: *Kindness.*

Tsao: That is right. *Kindness* is our magic word.

Emperor: Well, I am going to spread this word across the land. Perhaps then everyone in China can live in peace as you do.

[The Emperor leaves. Child 1 gets up and looks out of the door.]

Child 1:   Look at his beautiful carriage!

[All get up to look and exit.]

Grandfather: And to this day, every New Year's Eve, we try to make up with anyone we have fought with and be kind the whole year through.

Christine: But, Grandfather, it is very hard to be kind all of the time!

Grandfather: I know, but we must try in little ways with each other every day.

Kevin: Christine, I will share my dumpling with you. I am sorry I called you a liar.

Christine: Thank you, Kevin, I am sorry I called you a thief.

Grandfather: Tsao Wang would be proud of you, and so am I. Happy New Year!

Christine and Kevin: Happy New Year, Grandfather!

The End

Big Words, Strong Words
Teaching Notes

Background

Martin Luther King, Jr. always loved words. He learned to read at age four and joined the debating team in high school. At college, King studied the writings of Henry David Thoreau and Mahatmas Ghandi. Both of these men were willing to go to jail rather than obey unjust laws. King decided nonviolent, "passive resistance" was the answer to gaining equal rights for African Americans. When Rosa Parks, a black woman, decided not to give up her seat on the bus to a white passenger, she was arrested. So King and other leaders organized a successful bus boycott.

Using nonviolent methods in the face of brutality, King organized civil rights marches across the country. He inspired people with his speeches, and finally, in 1964, President Johnson signed the Voting Rights Act, giving every citizen the right to vote. King was awarded the Nobel Peace Prize that same year. He was the youngest person ever to receive that honor. The birthday of Martin Luther King, Jr. is now a national holiday. He is the only American who was not a president whose birthday is remembered in this way.

Extension Activities

Some Dreams

Talk with students about the difference between King's type of dream and a nighttime dream they may remember having. After establishing the difference between the two different dream types, encourage students to express their own personal hopes and dreams for their family, their country and the world. Have students illustrate their dreams. To create a class book, group the illustrated dreams into separate chapters (personal hopes, and dreams for family, country and world) and bind the pages together. Title the book "We Have Dreams."

Peacekeepers

Ask students to talk about situations that make them angry and the different ways they have to settle disputes with others. Record any and all possible solutions on a chart. Then, talk with students about how Martin Luther King, Jr. believed that the best way to settle arguments was peacefully. Return to your list and use a red marker to cross out those solutions students agree are not peaceful or positive. Ask students to consider the remaining items as a list of alternative behaviors they could try when they feel angry enough to strike back with harsh words or deeds. Post the list in the classroom and, when tempers run high, remind students to check the list before acting.

Big Words, Strong Words

by Bobbi Katz

Characters

- Narrator 1
- Narrator 2
- Mrs. Alberta King (King's mother)
- Christine (King's sister as a child)
- A.D. (King's brother, Alfred Daniel, as a child)
- M.L. (Martin Luther King, Jr. as a child)
- Mama Williams (King's grandmother)
- Martin Luther King, Sr.
- Martin Luther King, Jr. (at age 34)
- Crowd 1
- Crowd 2

Act 1

Narrator 1: If you ever go to Auburn Avenue, near the Ebenezer Baptist Church in Atlanta, Georgia, you'll find the boyhood home of Martin Luther King, Jr. Several generations of ministers have raised their families in that house. There's even a bronze plaque with the inscription: MARTIN LUTHER KING, JR. WAS BORN IN THIS HOUSE ON JANUARY 15, 1929.

Narrator 2: When he was born they called him M.L. At first he was like any other baby, cooing and crying. But soon, anyone could see that this little boy was growing into someone special.

The King family living room.

Mrs. Alberta King: Come along, children! It's time to leave for church. You know Daddy doesn't like us to be late.

Christine: But Mother, just look at the boys!

Mrs. Alberta King: M.L.! A.D.! Have you been fighting?

A.D.: It's all M.L.'s fault!

M.L.: Mother, A.D. says he's bigger and stronger than I am. But I'm six years old now—I just had to show him I wasn't afraid of him. We were just wrestling a little bit.

Mrs. Alberta King: *[sighing]* Now M.L., you should set a good example for your brother. Both of you, wash those messy hands and faces and change your shirts. Mama, will you please help these two little rascals?

Mama Williams: *[smiling]* Come along, children, let's go wash up. You don't want to miss a word of Daddy's sermon.

M.L.: *[changing shirt]* Mama, what is Daddy preaching about today?

Mama: I'm not sure, M.L. But I bet he'll be urging folks to stand tall—to be the very best they can be! And to meet hate with love.

M.L.: I love you, Mama.

Mama: I love you, too, M.L. Now we should get going before you and A.D. get into any more mischief.

[Later, same day. The whole family is at the dinner table.]

Martin Luther King, Sr.: Hmmm. Alberta, Mama, you sure know how to cook! Fried chicken, collard greens, sweet potato pies. Now this is what I call a feast fit for a king!

M.L.: *[teasingly]* That's why the King family is eating it!

Mama: *[laughing]* M.L. certainly has a way with words! He takes after his Daddy.

M.L.: [seriously] But Daddy has big words, strong words. When Daddy talks in church, people get all quiet trying to listen. Daddy, can you give me some of those words? Those big words?

Martin Luther King, Sr.: Son, you will have to find your own words. Grow, work hard, study, and you will find them.

M.L.: OK, I will! Mama, Daddy, Mother, A.D., Christine! Listen! I'm going to get words— big, strong words. Just you wait. I'm going to get them.

Act 2

Narrator 1: It's August 28, 1963, in Washington, D.C., and luckily, it's a beautiful day. More than 250,000 Americans from all over the country have come together in the spirit of peace. They have come carrying signs demanding equal rights for all Americans. Most of the people are black Americans. But there are many whites among them. Hand in hand, they march to the Lincoln Memorial.

Narrator 2: The leaders, who have been working hard for civil rights, speak to the sea of people. And then the man who had touched the hearts of fair-minded people throughout the world, comes to the microphone. He puts the speech he has written in his pocket. His words come from his heart.

Martin Luther King, Jr.: *[folding papers into his pocket]* Five score years ago a great American signed the Emancipation Proclamation . . . but a hundred years later . . . the Negro is still not free . . .

Crowd 1: Amen! Amen!

Martin Luther King, Jr.: I say to you my friends . . . I still have a dream. It is a dream deeply rooted in the American dream! I have a dream that one day this nation . . . will live out the meaning of its creed: We hold these truths to be self-evident; that all men are created equal. I have a dream!

Crowd 2: Amen! Amen! Oh yes, Amen!

Martin Luther King, Jr.: I have a dream that my four little children will one day . . . not be judged by the color of their skin . . . I have a dream today.

Crowd 1: Dream on! Dream on!

Crowd 2: *[cheering]* Amen! Dream on!

Martin Luther King, Jr.: I have a dream today! Little black girls and little black boys will join hands with little white girls and little white boys and walk together as sisters and brothers. I have a dream today!

Crowd 1: *[swaying to the rhythm of the words]* Yes! Yes! Dream on! Dream on!

Martin Luther King, Jr.: Let freedom ring from the . . . mountains of New York. Let freedom ring from the . . . Alleghenies of Pennsylvania. Let freedom ring from Stone Mountain of Georgia. Let freedom ring from Lookout Mountain of Tennessee. Let freedom ring from every hill . . . of Mississippi. Let freedom ring!

Act 3

Later that night in a quiet room.

Martin Luther King, Sr.: Remember when M.L. was little and used to say he was going to get himself some big words. Even then he knew how strong words can be.

Mrs. Alberta King: And he has found the strongest words of all—peace and love.

Martin Luther King, Sr.: I just hope the people listen with their ears . . . and their hearts.

The End

Dreaming of George and Abe
Teaching Notes

Background

George Washington, born on February 22, 1732, in Virginia, was Commander-in-Chief during the Revolutionary War and chairman of the committee that wrote the Constitution. In 1789, he became our nation's first president. The tradition of celebrating Washington's birthday began even before he became president. While Washington and his army were at Valley Forge, Pennsylvania in 1778, a small celebration took place at his headquarters during the frigid winter. Although his soldiers were hungry and cold, an army band marched and played for him.

The biggest Washington's birthday celebration took place in 1932, 200 years after his birth. Congress formed a committee to plan festivities that lasted from February to Thanksgiving.

In 1809, Abraham Lincoln was born in a log cabin in Kentucky and grew up on a farm. The family moved to Illinois in 1830. Lincoln had less than a year of formal schooling, but he was dedicated to educating himself. In 1861, Abraham Lincoln became the 16th President of the United States. He led the Union in the Civil War and signed the Emancipation Proclamation, which outlawed slavery in the United States. He served until he was assassinated in 1865. His story has inspired people of all ages. The first formal observance of Lincoln's birthday was held in the Capitol building in Washington, D.C., on February 12, 1866. In 1892, Illinois became the first state to make it a legal holiday.

Extension Activity

Memorable Memorials

• Bring in pictures of different landmarks dedicated to past presidents. The Lincoln Memorial, Washington Monument, Kennedy Space Center, and Mount Rushmore are some examples. Help students find the location of each landmark on a map. Discuss why monuments and memorials are built. Ask students to think of a person for whom they might want to build a monument. Have them draw pictures or use blocks and other building manipulatives to create models of their memorials.

• Provide students with a collection of various coins and bills. Before displaying the money, ask students if they know which President (or other famous face) is on each bill and coin. After students examine and identify the money, make a chart that shows who is on the bills and coins and what they are worth. Then offer students the chance to design money featuring someone they admire.

Dreaming of George and Abe

by Jim Halverson and Carol Pugliano-Martin

Characters

- Lisa
- Marci
- Connie
- Andrew
- George Washington
- Abraham Lincoln

Act 1

A classroom.

[The children enter.]

Lisa: So what are you guys going to do next Monday?

Marci: Go to school, of course. What a silly question!

Connie: Marci, we don't have school on Monday, remember? It's Presidents' Day.

Marci: Oh yeah. I forgot.

Andrew: I can't wait! It will be great to have an extra day to sleep late and play all day!

Marci: Is that why we have Presidents' Day?

Lisa: No. Presidents' Day is a special holiday to celebrate the birthdays of our two most famous presidents, George Washington and Abraham Lincoln.

Connie: That's right. And I've been thinking of something special we can do for the class. We should put on a Presidents' Day play.

Lisa: That's a great idea! I'll be Abraham Lincoln.

Andrew: And I'll be George Washington.

Marci: What can I be?

Connie: You can be the Narrator.

Lisa: What will you be, Connie?

Connie: The director, of course! Let's go to my house to work on it.

[They exit.]

Act 2

Connie's house.

[The kids are sitting around. They seem tired.]

Marci: Connie, we've been working on this play for hours. I'm getting tired.

Andrew: Yeah, Connie: Can't we take a break?

Connie: We want this play to be perfect don't we?

All: *[tiredly]* Yeah, yeah . . . but . . .

Connie: Then, let's try it again from the beginning. George Washington, you stand there. And Abraham Lincoln, you go there. Marci, stand up front and begin.

Marci: Welcome to our little play
All about Presidents' Day.
Our play is short and fun to see.
We'll start with George and the cherry tree.

[Marci steps back and Andrew, as George Washington, steps forward.]

Andrew: Once I got a brand new ax.
I loved it so, I couldn't relax.
I chopped at all that I could see
including my father's cherry tree.
When my dad asked me if I knew
who chopped the tree, what could I do?
I said, Dad, I cannot tell a lie—
I felled the tree, I don't know why.

Connie: Excellent! Now you go back to your place.

Andrew: Connie, are you sure that's why we celebrate George Washington's birthday? Just because he told the truth about a cherry tree?

Connie: Of course! I know all about George Washington: We eat cherry pie on his birthday, don't we?

Andrew: I guess so. But didn't he do anything better than just chop a tree down? I mean the whole country celebrates his birthday!

Connie: Never mind. OK, Abraham Lincoln, you're up next.

[Lisa, as Abraham Lincoln, steps forward.]

Lisa: When I was young, I was very poor.
I had no money, that's for sure.
I lived in a house that was made of logs.
We didn't have any cats or dogs.

Connie: Perfect.

Lisa: Connie, this is silly! So, Abraham Lincoln was poor. Is that why we celebrate his birthday? And who cares if he didn't have any cats or dogs?

Marci: Lisa is right. Being poor doesn't seem like much of a reason for Lincoln to be so famous.

Connie: Will you trust me? The play will be great. *[yawning]* You know, I'm kinda tired myself. I think I'll just lay down for a minute. I'll think better if I rest.

Andrew: *[lying down]* That's the best idea I've heard all day!

Lisa: Sounds good to me.

Marci: Me, too!

[They all lie down and are soon asleep. George Washington and Abraham Lincoln enter.]

Washington: So, Mr. Lincoln, what do you think of the play?

Lincoln: Well, Mr. Washington, it's cute. But I think Connie needs a little bit more information.

Washington: I agree. Let's talk to her.

[Washington and Lincoln approach Connie who is asleep. Lincoln gently nudges her.]

Connie: Wha . . . ? Huh . . . ?

[Connie screams and stands up abruptly. She and Lincoln are face to face. Lincoln tips his hat to her.]

Lincoln: Hello, Connie.

Connie: AHHH! Who are you?

Lincoln: I'm Abraham Lincoln. I'd like you to meet George Washington.

Washington: [shaking Connie's hand] How do you do?

Connie: [shocked] Hello. What are you doing here?

Washington: We heard about your play. We think you should know a little bit more about us before you continue.

Connie: You do?

Lincoln: Yes. It's true that George Washington here was a very honest man. But he did many other wonderful things that you celebrate on Presidents' Day.

Connie: Like what?

Lincoln: Well, Mr. Washington helped to make our country free. He also became the very first President of the United States. He's known as the Father of Our Country.

Washington: Well, thank you, Mr. Lincoln, my good man.

Lincoln: You're welcome. I've always been a big fan of yours, you know.

Washington: Well, thank you. But, Mr. Lincoln, you were a pretty great man yourself.

Connie: He was? What did he do?

Washington: Mr. Lincoln believed that all people should be treated equally, no matter what color their skin was. He helped to free the slaves.

Connie: Wow. That is great!

Lincoln: Well, we don't mean to brag. We just want you to put on a play that really helps other children learn facts about why they're celebrating our day.

Washington: Yes. The stories you tell in your play are fun, but they're not all that children should know.

Connie: Well, thanks for your help, Mr. Washington and Mr. Lincoln.

Lincoln: You're welcome. Now why don't you lay back down and finish your nap?

Washington: Yes, great playwrights need their rest. Good-bye!

[They exit. Lincoln leaves his hat behind.]

Connie: *[lying down]* Good-bye.

[The other children wake up.]

Marci: What a great nap!

Andrew: Yeah. I feel much better.

Lisa: Connie, wake up! Let's get back to work.

Connie: OK, Mr. Washington. Huh? Oh, you guys, you missed it! George Washington and Abraham Lincoln were just here!

Andrew: Oh, yeah? Right! Like we believe you!

Lisa: You must have been dreaming!

Connie: But it was so real. They told me all about themselves. Now that I know what great men they really were, I'm going to rewrite the play to tell about their great deeds!

Marci: Wow. What was it like to talk with them?

Connie: It was great. Too bad it was just a dream . . . *[She notices Lincoln's hat.]* . . . or was it? . . .

The End

An Earth Day Carol
Teaching Notes

Background

The first Earth Day was celebrated on April 22, 1970. Over the years, it has been commemorated in ways large and small. At the heart of any Earth Day observance is the knowledge that we must all work together to save our planet. Despite all of the gains since that first Earth Day, about one-third of the planet's biodiversity has been lost; forest cover is disappearing at a rate of about 6.5% per decade; and the world's population, currently about 6.75 billion, has nearly doubled, further taxing the planet's natural resources and adding to the problem of global warming. Earth Day is recognized as being needed now more than ever.

Extension Activities

Green Newsletter

Do an environmental audit of your school. Compile a list of things that students, teachers, and other school staff are already doing to help save the earth. Then make a list of actions that still need to be taken: Is litter being collected? Is there a lunchroom recycling program in place? Is water being conserved? Suggest that students work together to write up their findings and suggestions for future action. Compile their work into a environmental school newsletter and circulate it to all the classes (or deliver it by e-mail). The letter should applaud all efforts to date, and challenge everyone in the school to do even more.

Changes, Changes

Have students interview older adult family members to discover how their immediate environment was different when they were children. Develop a list of interview questions for the interviewees to answer, such as:

- Did you throw away as much garbage as we do now?

- How did you store food to keep it fresh?

- What happened when children outgrew clothing?

- How do you think the environment has changed over the years?

- What would you suggest to solve problems with the environment today?

Send a copy of the question list home with each child (or by e-mail), along with directions asking the interviewees to answer the questions and fill in their name and area they lived as a child, as well as the time period during which they lived there. Have students share the results of the interviews in class. What kinds of environmental changes for the better or worse have occurred? What work still needs to be done?

An Earth Day Carol

by Paula Thomas

Characters

- Narrator
- Ebenezer Litterbug
- Children 1–8
- Ghost of Earth Day Past
- Native American Boy
- Native American Girl
- Ghost of Earth Day Present
- Speaker
- Ghost of Earth Day Future

Act 1

Narrator: It was the day before Earth Day
And all through the town
No litter was anywhere,
Not uptown or down.

**Ebenezer
Litterbug:** *[walking along, kicking a can, garbage is hanging out of his pocket.]* Bah, Earth Day!

Child 1: Hey! Ebenezer Litterbug! Tomorrow is Earth Day. The whole town has been cleaning for weeks. Pick up your garbage!

**Ebenezer
Litterbug:** Mind your own beeswax! What do we pay street cleaners for?

Child 2: Looking after the environment is everybody's business, Ebenezer. That is what Earth Day is all about.

Ebenezer: Earth Day! Bah, Earth Day!

[Both children throw their hands up in frustration and walk off in opposite directions.]

Act 2

Ebenezer's bedroom.

Narrator: Ebenezer Litterbug lay asleep in his bed
Sorry fellow, there was much to dread.

**Ghost of
Earth Day Past:** *[carries a leafy tree branch to Ebenezer's bed, leans over and taps his shoulder]* Rise and shine, Ebenezer baby!

Ebenezer: *[sitting up with a start, rubbing his eyes]* Who are you?

**Ghost of
Earth Day Past:** I am the Ghost of Earth Day Past. You are making a mess of the Earth. You need a lesson. Come!

[Ebenezer gets out of bed and follows the Ghost to a woodland area.]

Ebenezer: Where are we? This is awesome, clean and green!

**Ghost of
Earth Day Past:** We are in America in 1492. This is how our country looked before wasting and polluting became the ways of the land.

[Native American boy and girl walk past and stop.]

**Native American
Boy:** Father says we must respect the earth.

**Native American
Girl:** If we treat her well she will reward us with food and all that is good.

[Boy and girl exit.]

**Ghost of
Earth Day Past:** All things here were pure and clean because the people took care of the earth. We must leave now.

[Ghost leads Ebenezer back to his bedroom.]

**Ghost of
Earth Day Past:**   Wait for the next ghost. See you around
Ebenezer buddy!

Ebenezer: *[waving]* Bye!

[Ebenezer lays down and the ghost exits.]

Act 3

Ebenezer's bedroom.

Narrator: Ebenezer was tossing
And turning in bed
Wondering: *Where's the next ghost?*
What lies ahead?

**Ghost of
Earth Day Present:**   *[walks to Ebenezer's bed, leans over, and takes
the covers off]* Wake up sleepyhead. We've got
to make tracks out of here. *[He beckons with
his finger to follow quickly to a recycling center.]*

Ebenezer: Who are you?

**Ghost of
Earth Day Present:**   I'm the Ghost of Earth Day Present. Follow me.

[The two walk together to a recycling center.]

Ebenezer: Why are we here?

**Ghost of
Earth Day Present:**   Look, listen, and learn.

[A group of children are standing as a speaker is talking.]

Speaker: The first Earth Day was on April 22, 1970. Earth Day is a day to enjoy our planet, learn about our planet, and help our planet. What can you do to help the earth?

Child 3: Don't throw out your cans, glass, plastics, or papers. Recycle!

Child 4: Throw your garbage in a trash bin. Don't litter!

Child 5: Don't waste water. Fix leaky faucets. Turn the water off while you're brushing your teeth.

Child 6: Walk, use the bus, or carpool. Energy is precious. Turn off lights and turn the heat down. Use it, and we'll all lose it!

Child 7: Reuse your shopping bags, plastics, and aluminum foil. Always try to use things more than once.

Child 8: Recycle your toys, books, and clothes. Give them to children who need them.

Ebenezer: These kids really think that they can make a difference.

Ghost of Earth Day Present: *[walking back to Ebenezer's bedroom]* You had better hope so, Ebenezer. We are all depending on it. The next ghost will come to show you why.

Act 4

Ebenezer's bedroom.

Narrator: Ebenezer waited.
Could he not guess?
He was about to see
One huge mess!

[Ghost of Earth Day Future goes to Ebenezer's bed, taps his shoulder and walks away.]

Ebenezer: Hey, wait! Who are you? *[He jumps up and runs after the Ghost to a vast wasteland. They stop to look around.]*

Ghost of Earth Day Future: I am the Ghost of Earth Day Future. I live here where there are no living things, only garbage and pollution.

Ebenezer: ARGHH! This can't be! I'm out of here! *[runs to hide under his blanket]*

[Ghost exits.]

Act 5

Ebenezer's bedroom.

Narrator: Ebenezer rose,
With just one thought in his head:
*It's Earth Day, by golly,
I'm not staying in bed!*

Ebenezer: *[jumping up and running to a group of children at the park]* Happy Earth Day, everyone!

Child 1: Is that you Ebenezer Litterbug?

Ebenezer: Yes, it's me, but I've changed!

Child 2: Are you going to stop littering and polluting?

Ebenezer: Yes!

Child 3: Are you going to follow the three R's and always reduce, reuse, and recycle?

Ebenezer: Yes! Yes!

Child 4: Are you going to live in the spirit of Earth Day and take care of the world?

Ebenezer: Yes! Yes! Yes!

All: *[to the tune of "We Wish You a Merry Christmas"]*

We wish you a Happy Earth Day,
We wish you a Happy Earth Day,
We wish you a Happy Earth Day,
And Recycling Day, too!

We will not waste or litter
Wherever we go.
We will help Mother Nature
And we'll all live and grow!

[Repeat refrain.]

The End

Becoming a Butterfly
Teaching Notes

Background

There are anywhere from 15,000 to 20,000 species of butterflies in the world, which scientists have grouped into families, according to their physical features. There are 725 species that frequent North America. Your students may have seen the beautiful monarch butterfly. In fact, this is probably the one that first comes to mind when children hear the word *butterfly*.

A butterfly goes through four stages of development, called *metamorphosis*. A butterfly deposits an egg on a leaf that will provide food for the caterpillar, or larva, that will emerge. After eating enough to grow to its full size, the caterpillar becomes a pupa by attaching itself to a sheltered, high spot, such as a branch or twig, and deposits a sticky liquid to fasten itself there. It then forms a hard shell around itself called a chrysalis. Inside the chrysalis, the larval structures transform into those of a butterfly. The pupa stage usually lasts one to two weeks. About an hour after the butterfly emerges from this shell, it is ready to fly.

Extension Activities

But Is It a Butterfly?

Invite students to form two groups to research the differences between moths and butterflies. Have students make construction-paper moths and butterflies for recording fast facts. Groups can display their shapes on a bulletin board. Since most butterflies are active during the day and most moths are active at night, you might divide the board in half, the butterfly half covered with yellow paper representing day, and the moth half covered with black, representing night.

That's a Long Trip!

Invite a group of students to research the migration of Monarch butterflies. Provide a large outline map of North America on which they can draw the routes the butterflies take and note the times of year when these migrations take place. Students can add illustrations to the map to show the butterflies themselves, the places where their eggs are laid, and the milkweed plants the larvae and adults use for food. Challenge students to calculate the mileage covered by the migrating butterflies on both legs of their fantastic journey.

Becoming a Butterfly

by Tara McCarthy

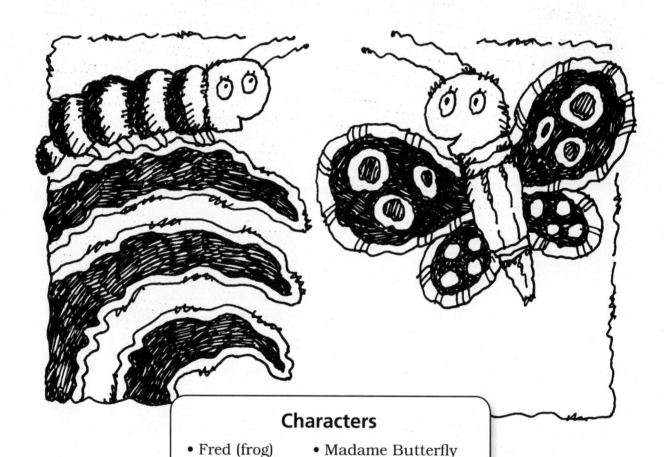

Characters

- Fred (frog)
- Phoebe (bird)
- Jay (bird)
- Robin (bird)
- Madame Butterfly
- Wiggles (caterpillar)
- Stripes (caterpillar)

Act 1

A warm day in early spring. The egg is lying on the leaves. Fred is sitting next to it.

Fred: Harumph! Harumph! Every spring I find a whole lot of these eggs. Madame Butterfly just plops them on leaves and flies away! Now I ask you, what kind of parenting is that?

[The birds come flying in and head for the egg.]

Phoebe: Hey, look guys! What a yummy morsel to eat!

Jay: Let me at it! I'm starving!

Fred: Hold on there! This is one egg you're not going to eat. Not while ol' Fred's here to stand guard!

Robin: Oh, come on, Fred! It's just an *egg*!

Fred: Harumph! Harumph! A lot you know! In a very short while, this egg is going to be a caterpillar. *[Stripes crawls on a branch and starts to nibble a leaf.]* Just like that caterpillar over there!

Phoebe: Even better! Caterpillars are even tastier than eggs. *[She heads for Stripes; Stripes looks up, scared.]*

Fred: Phoebe! Keep your beak off that caterpillar! In a few days, that caterpillar is going to be a pupa. Now you go right on eating, Stripes. I'll take care of you. *[Stripes continues nibbling.]*

Jay: Egg, caterpillar, pupa! Whatever are you croaking on about, Fred?

Robin: A thing by any other name tastes just as good, Fred!

Fred: Well this thing is a surprising thing! And you're in for the surprise of your life, because the pupa is going to be a BUTTERFLY!

[The birds all burst into laughter.]

Phoebe: A butterfly! You've gotta be kidding! *[Madame Butterfly comes flying in, humming a little tune.]* You mean that wiggly, ugly little crawly blob is going to be a gorgeous creature like that?

Madame Butterfly: Oh, yes, indeed. This *[pointing to the egg]* is my youngest child, and this *[pointing to Stripes]* is my eldest. I started off life in the very same way.

Fred: Harumph! Well, you might stick around and help me guard these kids of yours!

Madame Butterfly: I can't stick around. I have to collect nectar. It's what I eat, you know. *[She flies away.]*

Jay: *[grumbling]* Well, we're going to stick around, because we don't believe a word of any of this! Egg, caterpillar, pupa, butterfly. What a lot of nonsense!

Act 2

A few days later. The egg is gone, and Wiggles has taken its place. Wiggles is nibbling a leaf. Stripes is hanging on a twig.

Robin: *[surprised]* Well, I never in all my born days saw such a thing! That lumpy little egg did hatch into a caterpillar!

Fred: Harumph! Stick with me, and you'll learn a lot, kiddo!

Phoebe: *[excited]* Oh, look at Stripes! He's turning all green and shiny!

Wiggles: What's happening to my brother?

Fred: Don't worry! I told you that was going to happen. Stripes is becoming a pupa. He's forming a hard shell, called a chrysalis, around himself.

Robin: What a terrible fate! From a nice little crawly thing with legs to a quiet little blob . . . I mean pupa . . . hanging very still.

[Stripes is making little surprised noises. These continue softly while the other characters talk.]

Stripes: Ooh . . . ahh . . . wow . . . look at that . . . hmm! . . . what next? . . . ouch . . . whee! . . . it's dark in here! . . . not too roomy! . . .

Fred: Harumph! Inside that little chrysalis, a lot is happening. Stripes, the caterpillar, is turning into a butterfly. Parts of his body will change into whole different parts. Only his inside parts will stay the same.

Phoebe: Well, guys, shall we wait for a week to see the final act?

Robin and Jay: We wouldn't miss it for the world!

Fred: Just you wait and see!

Act 3

A week later. The birds and Fred are staring in the direction of the leaf where Wiggles was. Wiggles has disappeared. Another egg is on a leaf.

Stripes: Finished! Done! Look out, world, here I come!

Fred: Get ready for a beautiful surprise!

[Stripes is now a butterfly, moving and fluttering his wings. The birds flop onto the ground in amazement.]

Birds: Wow! . . . Fantastic! . . . the greatest! . . .

Stripes: I agree! Now I'm off to gather nectar.

[He flies away.]

Jay: No, come back, come back!

Robin: He didn't even say good-bye to his brother!

Phoebe: Where is Wiggles, anyway? Oh, my! *[She points at the egg.]* Wiggles turned back into an egg!

Fred: Harumph! Don't be silly! You know that's not the way it happens!

Jay: Yes, don't be silly, Phoebe! That's not Wiggles. But that egg will become a caterpillar, too . . .

Robin: . . . and the caterpillar will become a pupa, and . . .

[Wiggles, now a pupa, hangs on a nearby branch.]

Wiggles: That's me, folks! I'm a pupa today, but by and by . . . .

**Fred
and Birds:**   You're going to be a butterfly!

[Wiggles flutters out as everyone applauds.]

The End

A Kindness Returned
Teaching Notes

Background

The first seven days of May are set aside for a very special event: Be Kind to Animals Week! From guppies to Great Danes, tarantulas to tabbies, all sorts of pets are known to have a positive effect on people of all ages. As loving companions, built-in alarm systems, and antidotes for boredom and even depression, they can be demanding, heroic, mysterious, and comical. Mostly, they absorb our affection and return it tenfold.

Extension Activity

The Best Pets
Share the following chant with your students:

CHORUS:
If I had a pet, pet, pet,
Which one would I get, get, get?
If I had a pet, pet, pet,
To care for and to play with.

For a puppy of my own,
I would find a juicy bone.
Walk my puppy every day,
Teach it how to fetch and stay!

REPEAT CHORUS

For a kitten I would bring
A playful little ball of string.
Pour some milk into a cup,
Watch my kitty lap it up.

REPEAT CHORUS

For a fish I'd have a tank,
Making sure it ate and drank.
Feed it daily once or twice,
Change the water, keep it nice!

REPEAT CHORUS

For a bird I'd bring some seed,
And a cage the bird would need.
Listen as it chirped its song,
Sing out birdie, all day long!

REPEAT CHORUS

—by Meish Goldish

After you've read and enjoyed the poem, encourage students to innovate on the poem, inserting names of other possible pets, and creating rhyming verses. Then invite students to share their thoughts about what animals they think make the best pets. Have students each pick a favorite pet and generate a list describing the pet's attributes. Then ask them to use their list to write advertisements that try to persuade people to adopt this kind of pet from an animal shelter.

A Kindness Returned

by Robin Bernard

Characters

- Narrator
- Pam
- Dad
- Stephie
- Adam
- Mom

ACT 1

Kitchen of the Williams's home, winter.

Narrator: The Williams have just moved from an apartment into a house. Although moving was a big job, the family is happy to be in their new home and are busy unpacking.

[Pam comes in the kitchen carrying something inside her jacket.]

Pam: Look, everybody! Look what I found near the garbage cans! Poor kitty, she's so *skinny*! Can we keep her, Mom? Can we, Dad?

Dad: Well . . .

Stephie: *[rushing to look]* She's *cold* and *wet*!

Adam: *[rushing to look]* She must be *starving*!

Pam: And she has no collar!

Children: *Please*, can we keep her?

Mom: We'll see. But first, *[looking at the cat in Pam's arms]* we better get her warm and fed. Here's a towel, Pam. You dry her off while I get a saucer of milk.

Stephie: I'll find something for her to eat.

Adam: I'll make a bed for her!

Dad: And I better call the police and animal pound to see if anybody has reported losing a cat.

ACT 2

Two weeks later. The family is at the kitchen table eating dinner.

Stephie: *[looking at the cat]* Cleo looks so good, Mom. She must like your cooking! Her coat is shiny, and she's not skinny anymore.

Pam: Listen to her purr. She's so happy here!

Adam: *[speaking to his father]* We are going to keep her, Dad, aren't we?

Dad: Probably Adam, but we can't be sure for another few days. If nobody answers the ad we put in the newspaper, Cleo will officially belong to us.

[The telephone rings. Pam answers it.]

Pam: *[drops the phone receiver and runs out of the room crying]* No! It's not fair! Cleo is OUR cat!

[Stephie and Adam hurry after Pam.]

ACT 3

Later, the same night.

Adam: But I don't *want* to give Cleo away! How do we know they'll take good care of her?

Stephie: How do we know they'll feed her enough?

Pam: How do we know they'll love her as much as we do?

Mom: All of you—just listen. The Nelsons moved here just two weeks before we did and Muffin—our Cleo—got lost the very first day. That's why she was so skinny when Pam found her. And their little girl has been crying ever since because she misses her cat so much. Just try to imagine how she feels.

Pam: We don't have to imagine, Mom. We'll feel just as bad when they come to take her back.

Dad: I know it hurts to give up Cleo, but she belongs to the Nelsons. They've been worried sick about her and were afraid they might never see her again. We have to give Cleo back to her family; that's where she belongs.

[The children sadly nod their heads and leave the room.]

ACT 4

Two months later. Mrs. Williams is looking out of the kitchen window. The children come in from school.

Mom: Don't take your coats off, kids. We have a party to go to.

Adam: A party?

Stephie: Whose party?

Pam: Is it a birthday party?

Mom: Yes—and it's for *triplets*!

Children: *Triplets*!?

Mom: Well, furry triplets. Mrs. Nelson called this morning to thank all of you. She said if you hadn't taken such good care of Muffin, she never would have had such healthy kittens!

Children: *Kittens!?*

Mom: Three of them . . . six weeks old today, and there's one for each of you!

[The children cheer, and rush out the door with their mother.]

The End

Betsy Ross,
Seamstress With a Mission
Teaching Notes

Background

Flag Day is celebrated on June 14th in commemoration of the day the Continental Congress adopted the nation's first flag. Did Betsy Ross make this flag? Most historians say no, because the claim cannot be verified. Still, the story persists as a legend. It was first brought to the nation's attention by Betsy Ross's grandson, William Canby, who heard the family story from his Aunt Clarissa, Betsy's daughter. Canby presented the charming flag story to the Historical Society of Pennsylvania in 1870. The story later appeared in *Harper's* magazine and was soon being taught to schoolchildren across the country. Whether or not the story is true, there's no doubt that Betsy Ross was a real person. She was born Betsy Griscom in Philadelphia in 1752. Betsy was a gifted seamstress and worked as an apprentice at an upholsterer's shop, where she met John Ross. They later married and opened a shop of their own.

Extension Activity

Flag Day

Prepare for a celebration of Flag Day on June 14 with these suggestions.

- Challenge students to make a flag for your class or school. Team up pairs of students to work together cooperatively, just as Betsy Ross and George Washington did to design the first Stars and Stripes!

Washington's original sketch

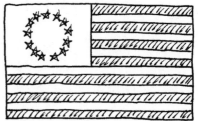

Ross' revised sketch

- Betsy Ross didn't keep a journal, but what if she had? What would she have recorded on that day in May, 1776, when she met George Washington? Encourage students to write imaginary entries for Betsy's diary.

- Have groups of students brainstorm ideas for a commemorative song or poem honoring Betsy Ross and her flag.

Betsy Ross, Seamstress With a Mission

by Eve Spencer

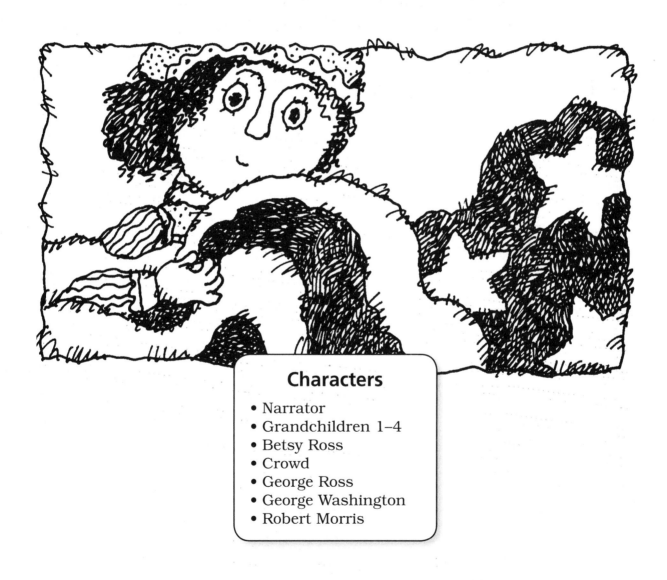

Characters

- Narrator
- Grandchildren 1–4
- Betsy Ross
- Crowd
- George Ross
- George Washington
- Robert Morris

Act 1

Philadelphia, Pennsylvania, 1825, at the home of Betsy Ross.

Narrator: Betsy Ross was born in 1752 and lived most of her life in the city of Philadelphia. She was an excellent seamstress and owned a sewing and upholstery shop for many years. Betsy Ross is remembered mostly for sewing our nation's first flag. It is a story that Betsy herself liked to tell her children and grandchildren.

Grandchild 1: Tell us a story, Grandma Betsy.

Grandchild 2: Yes, Grandma, a story!

Betsy: Certainly! What story would you like to hear?

Grandchild 3: Tell the story about the flag—

Grandchild 4: And the day you met George Washington!

Betsy: Ah, yes. That was an extraordinary day. An extraordinary time, really. It was the time when our country was newly born and fighting to survive.

Grandchild 2: When was that, Grandma?

Betsy: Well, let's see. It was almost 50 years ago, in 1776. I was 24 years old then. My husband John had recently died in an accident.

Grandchild 1: You must have been really sad, Grandma.

Betsy: Oh, I was terribly sad.

Grandchild 3: And you had to run your sewing shop all by yourself, didn't you?

Betsy: That's right, darling. I was trying very hard to keep my business open. But work was slow. The war against England was being fought, you know. I was worried I might have to close the shop. Until one day that spring, when my uncle, Congressman George Ross, came into my shop . . .

Act 2

May 1776, inside Betsy's sewing shop in Philadelphia.

Betsy: *[speaking to herself]* Hmmm . . . These shirt ruffles are tricky to make . . . *[hears noise, looks up]* . . . What's that commotion outside?

Crowd: *[murmuring]* It's him! It's him! It's General Washington!

[George Ross, George Washington, and Robert Morris enter.]

George Ross: Good afternoon, Betsy.

Betsy: Why Uncle, hello!

George Ross: Betsy, I'd like to introduce General George Washington from Virginia, the commander-in-chief of our continental army, and Robert Morris, my fellow Pennsylvania congressman.

Betsy: *[somewhat flustered]* Oh, my! Well, it's a great, great honor, sir, to meet you, General Washington, sir, and you, Congressman Morris.

**George
Washington:** Pleased to meet you, Mrs. Ross.

Robert Morris: How do you do, Mrs. Ross?

**George
Washington:** Mrs. Ross, I was terribly sorry to hear about the death of your husband. I know times must be hard for you right now. But we have a great favor to ask. And it must be kept secret!

Betsy: A secret? Well, I can certainly keep a secret.

**George
Washington:** Good! Your uncle told me you were trustworthy. He also said you were the best seamstress in Philadelphia. So that's why we want you to make a flag.

Betsy: A flag?

**George
Washington:** Yes, Mrs. Ross, a flag! Our thirteen colonies have joined forces to fight a war for independence. Together we'll win the war, and together we'll form a new nation. And our new nation needs a symbol—a flag—to bring all of us together as Americans. Will you make it?

Betsy: I'm very honored to be asked, sir. But I don't know if I can—

Robert Morris: Don't worry about the money, Mrs. Ross. We'll give you all you need.

Betsy: Oh, it's not the money, sir. It's just that I've never made a flag before. But if you wish, I . . . I can try.

George Washington:	Good! Now take a look at this sketch I made. *[He pulls out a sketch of flag.]* What do you think?
Betsy:	*[looking thoughtfully at the sketch]* Oh, that's a lovely flag, General, sir. It's very . . . square.
George Washington:	Well, yes. Most flags are square, Mrs. Ross.
Betsy:	*[shyly]* Yes, I guess they are. But take a look at these stripes, General. Maybe they'd seem bolder and brighter if they were longer?
George Ross:	Betsy, I'm sure the General doesn't want to hear . . .
George Washington:	No, she has an interesting point. Longer stripes would look better.
Betsy:	I like the idea of having 13 stars and 13 stripes.
George Washington:	Yes, I thought that would be nice. You know, one star and one stripe for each of the 13 colonies.
Betsy:	But what about the stars, General? Do you think they would look nicer if they were arranged in a shape? I don't know—maybe something round?
George Washington:	Hmmm. Maybe the stars should be in a circle. Yes, that might work!
Betsy:	*[boldly]* And what if the stars had five points instead of six? I think five-pointed stars look better.

George Washington:	I think so, too. But aren't five-pointed stars hard to make?
Betsy:	Actually, General, a five-pointed star is very easy to make.
George Washington:	It is?
Betsy:	Oh, yes. Here, let me show you. *[folds a piece of fabric and cuts it using scissors]* I can make it with just one snip of the scissors. Look, a perfect five-pointed star.
George Washington:	Amazing!
Robert Morris:	Just *one* snip!
George Ross:	Betsy, that's very nice, but I'm sure the General has given a lot of thought to his design.
George Washington:	Well, actually, I've been very busy lately. And your niece has made some good suggestions. Let me see if I can make a new sketch using her ideas. *[sits down, redraws the flag, then holds up the new sketch]* What do you think?
Betsy:	Perfect!
George Washington:	Then this will be the flag you'll make.
Betsy:	I'll get started right away.

George Washington: Excellent! I must say it's been a real pleasure meeting you, Mrs. Ross. Your suggestions were a great inspiration. Thank you.

Betsy: *[greatly pleased]* Why, thank you, sir!

[The three men say good-bye and leave.]

Narrator: Immediately after the men left her shop, Betsy started working on the flag. She bought the materials she needed and even borrowed a flag to study how it was made. And in a very short while, the flag was completed and approved. George Washington and the others liked it so much that Betsy received a contract to continue making flags for the government.

Act 3

Philadelphia, Pennsylvania, 1825, at the home of Betsy Ross.

Betsy: And that was the beginning of my flag-making business!

Grandchild 4: Grandma, why was the flag a secret?

Betsy: Well, dear, those were dangerous times. We were at war. It would have been terrible if the English had known about it.

Grandchild 2: Are you a hero, Grandma?

Betsy: Well, dear, I've heard some say that's so. But I feel I was just doing what I could to help our new country.

Grandchild 1: Grandma, that's a great story. I'm going to tell it to my own children and grandchildren some day.

Betsy: That would be wonderful, darling. But promise me something, all of you. Promise me that one day you will all be something special in your own lives. It doesn't have to be something big, just something meaningful. And then you'll have your very own stories to tell your grandchildren. Will you try to do that?

All grandchildren: We will!

Betsy: Good. Now, it's getting late, so let's say goodnight.

All: Goodnight!

The End

Summer Dreams
Teaching Notes

Background

Summer can be a glorious time for students to look forward to, but it also is a time that can signal uncertainty and change. After all, the freedom of summer brings an end to some comfortable home-away-from-home routines that were created during an entire school year. It means saying good-bye to a familiar past and hello to an uncertain future. For many students, the beginning of summer is a bittersweet time of letting go and moving on. For teachers, the awareness that students may be struggling inside can go a long way toward helping them make a smooth and happy transition out of the classroom and into the sunshine.

Extension Activities

See How We've Grown!

Students of any age benefit from seeing how far they've come and noting all they've accomplished during the school year. To this end, you can easily use your plan book as the basis for helping to create a class field trip down memory lane. Before school comes to a close, set aside time to go back through the pages of your lesson plans and make a list of all the learning experiences you shared together. For example, you might include some of the theme units you covered, all the songs you sang, poems you enjoyed, and the skills students mastered together. In addition, pull out some of your class photos, including pictures of displays and projects students worked on throughout the year. Then set aside time for a "remember when . . . " session. Present your memories and memorabilia and then invite students to add some of their own best memories to the mix. Finish by having each student write and illustrate one page for a class book titled "Our Class Memories." Make photocopies of each page—plus a blank page simply titled "Autographs" so that each student can own a copy of the book for classmates to sign.

Booking the Summer

Remind students of all the reading you've done together by compiling a list of the books and stories you've shared as a class. Then offer students a suggested summer reading list that builds on this foundation. For example, if in class students enjoyed a particular author, cite other books by that same author. If students read one of a series of books, recommend that they continue reading the rest of the titles. Finally, if students enjoyed a book that is available on film, suggest that they reread the book and enjoy viewing the movie.

Summer Dreams

by Jim Halverson

Characters

- Narrator
- Maria
- Christopher
- Lou
- Ghost of the School Year
- TV Set

Act 1

Maria, Christopher, and Lou walking home from school.

Narrator: Dreams of summer,
Dreams of play,
Dreams that school will go away.
Maria, Christopher, and Lou
Dream of what they're going to do
Once the long school year is through.

Maria: I can't *wait* for the end of school!

Christopher: I know! No more reading, no more spelling!

Lou: No more subtraction!

Maria: It's going to be wonderful. I'm not going to do anything except watch TV!

Christopher: I'm just going to play with my friends. I won't read a thing.

Lou: What I dream about is staying up as late as I want.

Maria: Nothing but TV! TV shows—More! Give me more!

Lou: It will be great. No school in the morning. I'll *never ever* go to bed!

Christopher: And no one will make me read a book!

[During this last speech the Ghost of the School Year sneaks up and sprinkles each of them with magical dust. The moment the dust covers them, the children fall into a dream of the future.]

Ghost: Let them hope.
Let them dream.
Things may not be as they seem.
I'm a wicked little haunt!
I'm going to give them what they want!
When they wake, they're going to see
The summer that they wished to be.

Act 2

Narrator: What was it that Maria wished for?
"TV shows—More! Give me more!"

[The TV enters. Following the TV is Maria, who seems to be dragged along as if she were a prisoner.]

TV: Happy to have you with us today, Maria.
This is your treat:
Lots of stuff,
Lots of stuff—
Time for a commercial—
Same old stuff!

Maria: Help! I've seen this all before. I'll change the channel.

[She points a remote control at the TV.]

TV: Happy to have you with us today, Maria.
This is your treat:
Lots of stuff.
Lots of stuff.
Time for a commercial—
Same old stuff!

Maria: You said that before. You're boring. I didn't really mean that I *only* wanted to watch TV. I mean, I did like lots of the things at school—

TV: School? School?
That's the word that rhymes with *fool!*

[Maria and TV exit.]

Narrator: Lou, you remember, clearly said,
"I'll *never ever* go to bed!"

[Lou enters, yawning and exhausted, and tries to get into bed. Every time he tries to lie down, the bed dumps him to the floor.]

Lou: I'm so sleepy . . . I just want to go to bed . . . Ouch, why can't I get into this thing? Oh, why did I ever wish such a silly wish?

[Lou exits.]

Narrator: Now let's see how Christopher looks.
He's the one who swore off books.

[Christopher enters.]

Christopher: *[angrily]* That's the last time I play with my brother! We always argue about what game to play. Then when we finally do get around to playing, he always tries to boss me around. I need some time to myself.

[He notices a pile of books.]

Christopher: I know I said I wouldn't want to read. But if I do, no one at school will ever know.

[He reaches for a book, but it moves out of reach. This happens a few times.]

Christopher: What's going on? Why can't I read? These books are acting just like my brother! I thought at least books would still be my friends. I wish I were back in school!

[Christopher exits.]

Act 3

The three classmates are in just the same positions as when the Ghost first sprinkled them with the magical dust.

Narrator: Maria, Christopher, and Lou
Have seen their summer dreams come true.

[The Ghost of the School Year enters, sprinkles them with dust again, and they awaken.]

Maria: Oh, I'm still here in school. I had the worst . . . I don't know what to call it. I hope it was just a dream!

Christopher: I dreamed that I really couldn't read all summer.

Lou: And I couldn't ever go to bed. I was so tired! It wasn't fun at all.

Maria: Watching TV all the time was like being in prison.

Christopher: Maybe vacation isn't going to be just what we thought after all.

Maria: And maybe school is OK.

Lou: I'm still going to have fun on vacation. But, you know, I'll probably look forward to coming back to school next fall, too.

[Enter Ghost of the School Year unseen behind them.]

Ghost: I'm going to teach them a little poem:
We like summer. We like school.
We think both are pretty cool.
In summer, we can laze and play,
And spend our days in different ways.
Fall means back to school, it's true.
But that's OK—we like learning, too!

Maria: We like summer. We like school.

Christopher: We think both are pretty cool.

Lou: In summer, we can laze and play,

Maria: And spend our days in different ways.

All: Fall means back to school, it's true.
But that's OK—we like learning, too!

The End

Notes

Notes

Notes